Wolf

Animal
Series editor: Jonathan Burt

Already published

Ant
Charlotte Sleigh

Ape
John Sorenson

Bear
Robert E. Bieder

Bee
Claire Preston

Camel
Robert Irwin

Cat
Katharine M. Rogers

Cockroach
Marion Copeland

Cow
Hannah Velten

Crow
Boria Sax

Dog
Susan McHugh

Donkey
Jill Bough

Duck
Victoria de Rijke

Eel
Richard Schweid

Elephant
Daniel Wylie

Falcon
Helen Macdonald

Fly
Steven Connor

Fox
Martin Wallen

Giraffe
Mark Williams

Hare
Simon Carnell

Horse
Elaine Walker

Lion
Deirdre Jackson

Lobster
Richard J. King

Moose
Kevin Jackson

Otter
Daniel Allen

Owl
Desmond Morris

Oyster
Rebecca Stott

Parrot
Paul Carter

Peacock
Christine E. Jackson

Penguin
Stephen Martin

Pig
Brett Mizelle

Pigeon
Barbara Allen

Rat
Jonathan Burt

Rhinoceros
Kelly Enright

Salmon
Peter Coates

Shark
Dean Crawford

Snail
Peter Williams

Snake
Drake Stutesman

Spider
Katja and Sergiusz Michalski

Swan
Peter Young

Tiger
Susie Green

Tortoise
Peter Young

Vulture
Thom Van Dooren

Whale
Joe Roman

Wolf

Garry Marvin

REAKTION BOOKS

Published by
REAKTION BOOKS LTD
33 Great Sutton Street
London EC1V ODX, UK
www.reaktionbooks.co.uk

First published 2012

Printed and bound in China by Eurasia

British Library Cataloguing in Publication Data
Marvin, Garry.
    Wolf. – (Animal)
    1. Wolves. 2. Wolves – Control – History.
    3. Wolves in literature.
    4. Wolves – Folklore.
    I. Title II. Series
    599.7'73-DC22

ISBN 978 1 86189 879 1

Contents

Introduction 7

1 *Canis lupus* 11

2 Lupophobia 35

3 Lupicide 81

4 Lupophilia 119

5 Rewilding 172

Timeline of the Wolf 182

References 184

Select Bibliography 192

Associations and Websites 195

Acknowledgements 196

Photo Acknowledgements 197

Index 198

Introduction

Wolves have always evoked powerful responses from humans who have encountered them or imagined them. In a few societies, particularly those in which humans have hunted as a means of subsistence, they have been admired as fellow hunters. In the main, however, they have been feared and reviled creatures of the wilderness. In Western cultures wolves, more than any other animal, have been emblematic of the wild and particularly of the dangerous and threatening qualities of the wild. Humans have feared the wolf as a formidable pack hunter that could kill the largest of wild animals, attack domestic flocks and herds and even turn humans into prey, but the wolf has always been more than a carnivore pursuing a necessarily carnivorous life in a natural, morally neutral manner. Instead it has been characterized as rapacious, voracious, greedy, deceitful, murderous and criminal and, when its predatory attentions have turned to humans, a monstrous creature of vicious and evil intent. Humans, seeking to do harm to others, have cloaked themselves in images of the wolf as hunter or warrior while others who sought, or were compelled, to do harm in more malign ways became wolves – a transformation that was feared for centuries in Western cultures. Even early natural history tracts presented the wolf as a despicable creature. Comte de Buffon, for example, characterized the wolf as 'an enemy of all society' and finished his description thus:

A walk in the woods.

7

In fine, the wolf is consummately disagreeable; his aspect is base and savage, his voice dreadful, his odour insupportable, his disposition perverse, his manners ferocious; odious and destructive when living, and, when dead, he is perfectly useless.[1]

As a consequence of how the carnivorous ways of wolves entered into human concerns, human groups waged campaigns of extermination against the wolf and were successful in eradicating it from most of its territory. In much of Europe this was accomplished centuries ago, while in most of North America this happened only a generation ago. Once wolves were gone there opened up a cultural space, although still restricted geographically, into which a newly understood scientific wolf and a new wolf of the popular imagination emerged. The modern scientific wolf was no longer the reviled creature of early natural history texts. It was now understood to be a highly intelligent and complex social creature that posed no threat to ecosystems, and indeed was a benefit to those systems in which it still existed or to which it might be reintroduced. Alongside this wolf there emerged a new cultural wolf that was the mirror opposite of its previous image – a charismatic creature imbued with a spirit of a newly valued wilderness, a creature now adored as much as it had been previously demonized. But still, alongside this revaluing of the wolf, the image of an unwanted, rapacious, carnivore has persisted. For many whose lives depend on domesticated livestock or who wish to hunt the wild game on which wolves prey, the benign eco-wolf is a mistaken representation created by those who rarely, if ever, see the creature and for whom its predations have no consequences.

As a species, *Canis lupus* has been, until humans set about attempting to eradicate it, the world's most widely distributed

Illustration of a hanged man being eaten by wolves, front cover of *Le Petit Journal* (1906). There is a long history of wolves reputedly scavenging on human corpses.

8

Le Petit Journal

Le Petit Journal
CHAQUE JOUR — 6 PAGES — 5 CENTIMES
Administration : 61, rue Lafayette

Le Supplément illustré
CHAQUE SEMAINE 5 CENTIMES

5 Centimes **SUPPLÉMENT ILLUSTRÉ** 5 Centimes

Le Petit Journal Militaire, Maritime, Colonial..... 10 cent.
Le Petit Journal agricole, 5 cent. ‡ **LA MODE** du Petit Journal, 10 cent.
Le Petit Journal illustré de La Jeunesse..... 10 cent.
On s'abonne sans frais dans tous les bureaux de poste

ABONNEMENTS

	SIX MOIS	UN AN
SEINE ET SEINE-ET-OISE	2 fr.	3 fr. 50
DÉPARTEMENTS	2 fr.	4 fr. »
ÉTRANGER	2 50	5 fr. »

Les manuscrits ne sont pas rendus

Dix-septième année — **DIMANCHE 7 JANVIER 1906** — Numéro 790

DANS LA LANDE BRETONNE
Un pendu dévoré par les loups

wild/non-domesticated land mammal, apart from *Homo sapiens*. As a result wolves are creatures whose lives have intersected with a wide range of human societies and human cultures. This intersecting history has resulted in a vast literature and gallery of images of wolves, for the wolf has never been a creature that can be ignored. The wolf of this book is largely the wolf of Western cultures and Western imaginings and representations. It would be impossible for one book to capture the cultural history of wolves everywhere since such an account would run to several volumes. Here universality has been traded for cultural specificity, for an exploration of particular interconnections of wolf lives and human lives – a story of lupophobia and lupicide, but also of lupophilia.

1 *Canis lupus*

Before the first scientific field studies of wolves,
which did not begin until the early decades of the
twentieth century, the natural history of the wolf was
little known. What was known, or imagined, about
it came largely from local traditional knowledge or
through its representations in fables, folklore, travellers'
tales and other popular stories.[1]
David Mech, *The Wolf: The Ecology and Behaviour of an
Endangered Species*

Mammalian orders began to emerge and diverge in the
Paleocene epoch, some 65–55 million years BP. In the northern
hemisphere there emerged a group of meat-eating animals
known as Creodonts (Greek for 'having teeth for eating flesh')
from which the family of Carnivora developed. Towards the
end of this period there emerged a mammal with carnassial
teeth (the premolar teeth of carnivores adapted for tearing
through skin, muscle and tendons) named Miacis. From Miacis
two lines of mammals diverged, one of which, Cynodictis,
evolved into what was to become the dog family. This creature
had the same number of teeth as a modern wolf but was much
smaller. With the emergence of Cynodictis and the animals that
evolved from it, early signs of the characteristics of modern
wolves began to emerge.[2] These animals already had wolf-like
teeth but it was their legs and feet that were of significance in
their emergence as hunters: the legs became longer, the feet
longer and more compact, and the tail shorter, allowing them
to range widely and pursue prey at a regular pace over long distances. From Cynodictis emerged Cynodesmus and from that
creature emerged Tomarctus just over fifteen million years

ago. It was from Tomarctus that the wolf and the fox began their divergent evolutions.

The emergence of the *Canis* genus has been dated to the late Miocene period (4.5–9 million BP). By the late Pliocene period

(1.25–2.5 million BP) small forms of *Canis* were widespread in North America and the Old World; all wolves probably derived from these early canids. These early forms of wolves were not, however, the modern wolf and there were possibly nine wolf species before the emergence of *Canis lupus*. The first emergent wolf species, as we would recognize them, appeared between 2.5 and perhaps 1.8 million years ago. Some scientists have thought that *Canis priscolatrans* was a large, early coyote (*latrans* from this early creature is picked up in the naming of the modern coyote – *Canis latrans*), and that the wolf and coyote lineages diverged fro this period. Others, however, favour the argument that *Canis priscolatrans*, although small, was a true wolf of North American origin. These creatures then travelled back to North America in several waves, beginning some 400,000 years ago, across glacial ice or when sea levels in the Bering Strait made such migrations possible. As part of the evidence for these migrations of wolves between North America and Eurasia, some subspecies today on one continent seem to be more closely related to subspecies on the other than they are to subspecies on the same continent.[3]

Before the concerted attempts to kill and control wolf populations, largely over the last 500 years, wolves were found in historical times across the breadth of North America and from the high Arctic to northern Mexico. Their territories also extended throughout Europe, across the Middle East, south into the Arabian Peninsula and across Asia as far east as Japan.

The wolf was named *Canis lupus* by Carl Linnaeus in 1758. Intriguingly, Linnaeus chose *canis* (domesticated dog) rather than *lupus* (wolf) for the first part of his classificatory name. This order, literally 'dog wolf', suggests that 'dog' is the basic species, with 'wolf' secondarily related to that. Thus it could be interpreted that the wolf has 'gone wrong' – a wild creature developing out of a domesticated animal – rather than the dog being a domesticated *lupus*.[4] Scientists also debate whether this simple two-word name is enough to capture the complexity of the species. It has been suggested that geographic barriers in the vast areas occupied by wolves resulted in restrictions or breaks in the flow of genes across populations, which in turn resulted in morphological and genetic differences between populations of such significance that they warrant subspecies identifications. Arguments have been made for the recognition of 24 subspecies of *Canis lupus* in North America alone and some taxonomists have argued for the recognition of a further nine subspecies in Eurasia. Following analyses of a wide range of wolf skulls, however, one taxonomist has identified only five *Canis lupus* subspecies in North America (*arctos*, *occidentalis*, *nubilus*, *baileyi* and *laycaon*), with a fairly certain five subspecies in Eurasia (*albus*, *communis*, *lupus*, *cubanensis* and *pallipes*). Recent

'Loup', from Étienne Geoffroy Saint-Hilaire and Georges Frédéric Cuvier, *Histoire Naturelle des Mammifères* (1819–41).

'The Common Wolf (*Canis lupus*)', from Saint-Hilaire and Cuvier, *Histoire Naturelle de Mammifères*.

research also indicates that a small Italian wolf, named as *italicus*, might be a subspecies and that there might be a further four subspecies – *arabs*, *hattai*, *hodophilax* and *lupaster* – in different parts of Eurasia.[5]

Canis lupus is the largest of the wild canids but it is larger in the popular imagination, and particularly in popular graphic representations, than in the scientific record. In northern areas males average some 43–8 kg (95–106 lb), with few exceeding 54 kg (120 lb), and 36–42 kg (80–92 lb) for females, with few exceeding 48 kg (106 lb).[6] Wolves in southern zones, especially in arid or desert regions, are on average 50 per cent lighter than their northern relatives. Many writers refer to the largest recorded wolf as one weighing 79 kg (175 lb), which was killed in Alaska in 1938, and the largest recorded wolf in Eurasia as an 86-kg

Alexander Bell, 'Canis', from *Encyclopedia Britannica* (*c.* 1750–80), wood engraving depicting domestic dogs (*Canis familiaris*) and their wolf (*Canis lupus*) ancestor.

(189-lb) animal killed in Ukraine.[7] Wolves average a height of 65–80 cm (26–32 in) at the shoulder, although some individuals have measured up to 90 cm (36 in). Male wolves average between 150 and 200 cm (60–78 in) long from nose to tail and females 140–85 cm (55–72 in). So wolves are a little shorter than adult humans are tall. In comparison, a German Shepherd, a dog that many people think is wolf-like, weighs on average between 34 and 39 kg (75–85 lb), stands between 55 and 65 cm (22–6 in) at the shoulder and has a body length of between 60 and 72 cm (24–9 in).

Many popular writers on wolves quote with approval the Russian proverb '*Volka nogi kormyat*' (the feet feed the wolf).[8] This relates to how the legs and the feet of the wolf are of fundamental importance to how it feeds itself. Wolves must often range widely in search of potential food and the structure and configuration of their legs and feet allow them to move at a steady pace across great distances. The particular swinging wolf gait, with the fore and hind legs following in the same line (as compared with the domestic dog, which puts the hind foot to the side of the point where the fore foot lands), allows the creature to lope along at about 8–9 km/h (5–5½ mph) for many hours with few pauses.[9] There is considerable debate about how fast a wolf can run but a top speed of some 60 km/h (35 mph) in a short burst and about 39 km/h (24 mph) for a kilometre or so is a reasonable average. Most of any swift burst occurs when the wolf is actively hunting and attempting to close on fleeing prey, but however important its feet and legs are to bring it within reach of its prey, they are not much help in overcoming it.

When getting to grips with its prey the wolf depends on its teeth, particularly its canines. Stories and descriptions that emphasize the size of wolves' teeth are part of the image of the monstrous wolf but, in contradiction to the fairy tale, it is the

CANIS.   Plate CXIX.

King Charles's Dog.   Pyrame D.   Shock D.

Small Danish D.

Lion D.   Bastard Pug D.

Naked Turkish D.

Pug D.   Mongrel Turkish D.

The Wolf.

Mongrel Hound.

A.Bell Print at Sculptor fecit.

Wolf skulls, from
George Mirart,
*The Monograph
of the Canide.*

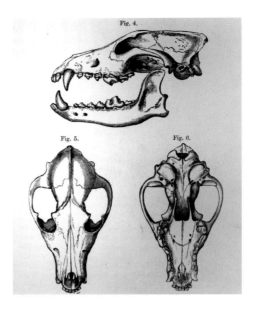

type and particular combination of their teeth rather than the size that is important. Wolves' incisors and canines, supported by a jaw that has a crushing power of some 1,500 lb/in^2 (double that of the largest domestic dog), are incredibly strong since, once locked on to a large prey, they have to withstand the forces generated by the struggling animal and to support the weight of the wolf, which may often be lifted off the ground as it attempts to remain attached. Unlike big cats, wolves do not attempt to leap onto their prey. Their non-retractable claws are blunt from direct contact with the ground and have no grip. Wolves must therefore get in close to their prey, to worry it, and slash at it with their canine teeth, or tear and bite it with their incisors. It is this opportunist biting, grabbing and pulling, and the multiple laceration of the animal with the resulting loss of blood, that finally brings it down. Once on the ground and immobilized the prey is often killed as it is being devoured. Here the carnassials, the molar and premolar teeth, come into operation for they are designed to shear through hide, flesh, tissues and tendons, to crush bones and grind flesh and bones.

The image of 'wolfing down' food is certainly applicable to the voracious feeding by wolves that might have gone without food for many days. A young moose or elk can be devoured in a few hours. Wolves need an average of some 3.3 kg (7⅕ lb) of meat a day and so they need to eat as much of their prey as possible. With large prey they can consume great quantities. The stomach capacity of an adult wolf is between 7 and 9 kg (15–19 lb) and they may consume up to 25 per cent of their body weight when feeding on a large carcass.

Wolf packs containing as many as 42 members have been recorded but the average is probably between three and eleven. The pack is the milieu in which the close intimacy and complexity

Pack pups chew on bison bones, Yellowstone National Park.

of wolf sociability is lived. The core of wolf social life is a mated pair, which forms the initial building block for a pack. A wolf pack is not a loose aggregation of individual animals that come together (unrelated wolves rarely join a pack), but rather a closely related group of animals that, except for the founding pair, were born together. They are also, although there are exceptions to this rule, siblings because generally only the founding pair continue to mate within the pack. Packs are therefore generated from within or become smaller through splitting.

If a pair of wolves mates successfully and have pups (an average litter would be between four and six pups) that survive to early maturity – between four and ten months – there will be the beginnings of a full pack life. The offspring may stay with the parents for anything between one and three years. Although social relationships within a pack may have an influence on

Artist unknown, 'Wolves', 1813, engraving published by John Wheble, London.

whether and when young adults might leave the home pack, it is more likely that the availability of prey within the pack's territory is the crucial factor determining its size. So, for example, if there is little potential food the parents may force their pups to disperse by denying them sufficient food. If, however, there is plenty then the pack is likely to grow: the now-mature young of the previous year will remain with their parents, who will produce pups the following year, and the pack will become a complex, cross-generational group of related siblings plus parents.

At first it is the mother that is responsible for new pups but soon after birth other members of the pack contribute to raising them. A few weeks before she gives birth in the spring, the pregnant female begins searching for and preparing a suitable den with other members of the pack often assisting with the digging. Dens are not always constructed anew and females may return several times to dens that have served them well in previous years. Although wolves make dens in a variety of places, most are created by digging out an underground chamber.

A typical den comprises an entrance wider than it is high and a tunnel (often sloping upwards so that water does not enter) up to 4 m (13 ft) long, leading to a chamber large enough for a female to move around and for her pups. While she is in the den with her pups she is unable to leave in order to hunt and her mate will supply her with food, either bringing meat to her or regurgitating it from his stomach. The young pups will stay in the den for some three weeks before they emerge and begin their pack life. There is a strong tendency for only the original pair to breed and their first litter of offspring contribute in various ways to looking after the pups. Young pups play with the adults and will also solicit food from them by licking their muzzles. If an adult has eaten, this licking will result in them regurgitating food for the pups. At this time the mother no longer

receives food from her mate and she must leave the pups and hunt for herself. She is able to do this because others in the pack will be alert to any danger the pups might be in when she is absent. After about eight to ten weeks, in late spring or early summer, when they are weaned, the young wolves are moved away from the den to a 'home site' or 'rendezvous site', of which there may be several in a mature pack's territory. These are generally open areas with good ground cover in which the young wolves can hide, and are reached by several paths by which the adults leave for, and return from, hunting. Such sites are the focus of pack activities during the summer and autumn, after which the maturing pups are able to join the adults in the nomadic hunting life in the winter.

Having only one breeding pair, with the more mature taking care of the less mature, might be interpreted as a form of individual and communal altruism for the benefit of all. However, young adults may possibly also gain from the experience of caring for young pups when they later mate and become parents. Some popular accounts of wolf life portray it as caring, cooperative family life that is only occasionally shaken by internal conflict. Wolf social life, however, is not one of an ever-extending family. That there is usually only one breeding pair in any pack does not mean that others have withdrawn voluntarily from the world of reproduction; rather, they have not had the opportunity to breed. Wolves may attempt to breed within the pack – something that involves competitive engagement with the original breeding pair – but most breed by leaving the original pack and young wolves generally leave the pack by the age of two. Those that leave may be, for a time, lone wolves but this does not reflect some preferred condition, nor are they the rugged, heroic individuals of popular legend. Rather, they are wolves looking for potential mates. If a lone male and a lone female do find one another, or if a lone male lures a female from another pack, and they find enough territory with potential food that is not already occupied by another pack, they may well breed and the whole wolf pack cycle will start again, promoting further wolf dispersal later.

The problem of finding unoccupied territory in which to establish a family is a most important one for dispersing wolves because wolf packs are intensely territorial. For wolves a territory is an area, demarcated by frequent scent-marking, hunted in by that pack and defended against incursion by other wolves. A newly formed pair will need to find enough space to form a territory without encroaching on the territory of another pack, unless they are willing to fight for it, and they will need to establish one many times larger than they need for their own subsistence because there will be a family to feed in the future. Such territories can vary enormously in size depending on whether there are other wolves close by and the availability of food. As extremes, a pack of six wolves in Minnesota occupied a territory of a mere 33 km² (13 sq. miles), whereas an Alaskan pack of only ten wolves had a territory of 4,335 km² (1,693 sq. miles).[10]

A wolf with its head held almost vertical, mouth slightly open and often silhouetted against a full moon, is a ubiquitous, perhaps iconic, image. Fear of and fascination with the howling of a pack of wolves is a matter of human concerns – a long-held fear that it might signal attack on them or their livestock or a more recent interest and delight in the haunting sounds of the wild. Howling might occasionally be directed at intruding humans but it mainly serves important wolf concerns. Wolf communication specialists point out that howling is used in contexts that are both competitive and communicative and may serve several functions relating to reunion, social bonding, spacing and mating.[11] Howling is a very effective form of communication at a distance and one that can function at day or night.

Wolf pack resting in deep snow, Yellowstone National Park.

Howls can carry up to 10 km (6 miles) in forested terrain and up to 16 km (10 miles) across tundra or other open terrain.

Inter-pack howling, rather than being a mechanism for demarcating territory, might best be understood as an avoidance mechanism so that rival packs do not encounter one another. If two packs do meet then smaller packs are reluctant to howl and draw attention to themselves, whereas larger packs will howl. In a situation of inter-pack howling wolves do not howl in unison but rather use differently modulated howls with changes of pitch. Complex disharmonies make it difficult for listening wolves to determine the possible size of the other pack: just a few wolves can give the impression of being many and so, at a distance and out of sight, a small pack can give the impression of being large. Whereas scent-marking along the peripheries

Wolves greeting as the pack rests, Yellowstone National Park.

of territories communicates complex information about the condition of individual members of a pack, howling conveys little precise information about the number in a pack or about the age, health or sex of its members. Unlike the situation when packs meet and can see one another, confrontation rarely follows howling interactions and it is perhaps the very ambiguity and uncertainty of this form of communication that makes wolves cautious, with a preference for avoidance.

Within packs wolves howl when they are separated, which suggests that they use howling for location and coordination. Although intra-pack howling has been interpreted as a form of communication that strengthens social bonds between pack members, some experts argue that there is no firm evidence for such an interpretation. They also note that the howling of separated wolves is constructed as a harmonious chorus, whereas when pack members are close such a chorus is disharmonious. This might suggest that when separated, wolves signal that they are linked as a group, whereas when they are physically close they signal their individuality.

Howling, even in a chorus, is a rather simple signalling system. The complexities of wolf social life are conducted and communicated through an amalgam of auditory, olfactory and visual signals. Young pups have a range of vocalizations that are termed squeal, scream, yelp and bark; they then develop the young adult sounds of the moan, whine, growl and bark, before developing the adult woof, squeak and howl. All these sound signals communicate and respond to immediate mood. Visual signals comprising a range of body postures, gestures and movements relating to calmness, fear, greeting and distancing, aggression, submission and sexual intention or rejection also communicate something immediate. They include facial expressions based on movements of the eyes, ears and mouth; the position and movement of the tail; and the postures of the entire body from upright, through semi-prone, to lying on the ground and rolling to one side or lying on their back with the belly fully exposed.

Wolves live in a multi-sensory social world in which members of the pack organize their lives through complex signalling of their individual emotional state and their physical being to others and their response to others' signals. All of these forms of communication have a purpose in wolf lives. Although wolves must be ever vigilant of incursions by other wolves, most of their daily life is directed outwards towards hunting possible prey and inwards to their own social life. Hunting is an almost continuous activity for the pack and they tend to be extensive hunters, travelling across their territory in search of prey, rather than exploring locally in great detail. Although wolves will prey on a range of small animals and will scavenge carcasses, they need large quantities of meat and therefore direct their attention towards large herbivores in their territory (and this includes domesticated livestock in many areas). On their travels wolves might simply encounter suitable prey, but it is also clear that they approach prey they cannot initially see by following scent. Wolves are able to scent some prey at a distance of more than a kilometre.

Wolves are strong, fast, can endure a long-distance chase and, in a pack, are powerful. The large animals on which they prey, however, are adapted to wolf behaviour – they are ever vigilant and swift in flight. Although wolves might chance upon a suitable animal, they prefer to stalk their prey, keeping out of sight as long as possible. Wolf biologists seem to agree that, wherever possible, wolves target and then test potentially weak and vulnerable individuals as part of their strategy. Some prey, such as smaller deer, can escape a wolf attack because they

are able to flee faster than the wolves. Others, such as elk, caribou, bison and musk oxen, present other difficulties for their predators since they are strong, have horns or antlers, can deliver a lethal kick or have sharp hooves. A pack attacking a large individual of this type may succeed in killing it and gaining a huge amount of food, but the risk is the potential for injury or even death to pack members. When the potential prey finally sees the approaching predator there are two main responses. First, it can flee, either on its own or in a herd. Modern biologists who have seen this phase of a hunt report that, if they do not isolate a suitable animal, wolves generally abandon their pursuit after a few hundred yards although a few have been recorded as covering more than a mile. During this short, fast rush wolves seem to look out for young animals that can be separated from their mothers or others that exhibit signs of weakness, for example lameness, and they direct their attack, if it comes, to them. The second response to approaching wolves is for the animal to stand and face its attackers. A relatively small and defenceless creature such as a deer is unlikely to be successful with this tactic and will quickly be attacked and killed, as will weak or ill animals. Large, strong, fit animals that stand their ground and parry any testing attacks by lunging with their heads and hooves can resist even a group of wolves. Wolves might leave such an animal after a few minutes, but stand-off confrontations have been recorded as lasting several hours. If it wishes to survive, an animal should not attempt to flee. Wolves will respond to such a tactic by rushing at the animal and attacking it from the sides

Wolves testing a bison for signs of weakness, Yellowstone National Park.

Wolves in pursuit of a bull elk, Yellowstone National Park.

and rear. In flight an animal is not easily able to defend itself and its chances of survival are poor.

The image of a pack of wolves working together to track down, encircle and then attack their prey illustrates the power and ruthlessness of wolves when hunting. The highly social and cooperative behaviour of wolves is also expressed in working together in hunting. Wolves clearly hunt collectively, but are they hunting collaboratively in the sense of using teamwork and tactics that involve each wolf being aware of what the others are doing and shaping and synchronizing its behaviour to fit with that of the others. Some research suggests that what appears to be cooperative and coordinated is little more than un-coordinated collective opportunism. Intriguingly, the scientific view that wolves hunt cooperatively might be the result of how wolves have been observed in the wild. Because of the difficulties for an observer on foot to follow an entire hunt, most observations of hunting have been from the air, where pursuits and attacks that might be haphazard or opportunistic have been interpreted as having the pattern of planning and strategy.[12]

Whether hunting is cooperative or simply collective, the apparently adaptive advantage of a large pack hunting large prey might not be an advantage at all. An individual mature wolf can kill even the largest prey animals, such as moose, in the right circumstances and a pack might consist only of the breeding pair with their maturing offspring, which – because of their limited strength and experience – would be little help with hunting. Wolves in a large pack that brings down a large animal will, individually, gain less meat for their effort than a pair of wolves. A large pack is not therefore necessary for wolves to hunt and it might need to have more successful hunts more often to sustain its members.

An early view, often repeated in popular scientific literature, presented the social organization of a wolf pack as that of cooperative behaviour within a strictly hierarchical structure of dominance and submission. At the top of the pack were the

Wolves harrying elk, Yellowstone National Park.

31

dominating patriarchal alpha male and the matriarchal alpha female. All others in the pack attained their place in the hierarchy by forcing others into submission and by submitting to others. Modern scientists suggest that such a model is overly deterministic and does not capture the shifting relationships between the pack members that constitute a family. David Mech, the doyen of wolf scientists, has admitted that in his early work, when little was known about wolf social organization, he contributed to this hierarchical model when he first used the terms 'alpha male' and 'alpha female'. He now argues for a very different model. The term 'alpha' suggested that individuals achieved a particular status through aggressive competition or because of inherited traits or innate characteristics. Mech and other scientists have come to understand that 'most wolf packs are merely family groups formed in the same ways that human families are formed', through the coming together of an unrelated male and an unrelated female from different packs.[13] Mech prefers

Intrapack activity.

the neutral terms 'breeding male' and 'breeding female' for the senior wolves that look after their pups and guide them through their territory as they become young adults. Wolves become leaders because they have experience and their offspring follow because they need to gain experience before setting off on their own as adults. Such a rethinking of the structures of wolf packs tones down the notions of violence and aggression to something less dramatic. In this new model, conflicts within the pack are configured as the result of intra-family squabbles rather than as struggles for power.

The bear and the wolf – two of the charismatic mega-fauna of the United States.

Beyond the scientific interest in wolf societies expressed in terms of breeding males, breeding females, offspring, unrelated adults and rival packs, wolf lives have been interpreted in terms of fathers and mothers, brothers and sisters, of families and societies, and of close kin and outside enemies. These latter terms create a perspective of human concerns reflected in wolf lives: that wolves live in cooperative families in which members other than the parents take part in feeding, care, discipline and protection; that they form strong individual and enduring emotional bonds; that breeding pairs are, in the main, monogamous; that social organization is quasi-democratic and that food is obtained cooperatively and shared communally. The hierarchical model focuses on a quasi-political system of discipline, leadership and subordination. Related to such conceptions of leaders and followers is the notion of allegiance and its associated ideas of duty, responsibility, loyalty, emotional support and bonding. Within the family structure the image is of aggression and conflict being carefully managed but, when faced with a threat from outsiders, wolves respond aggressively and violently to defend their territory against others that seek to intrude.

Such images of human-like wolves do not only open up the possibility of thinking about wolf-like humans: they also show how scientific ideas can never fully be separated from cultural ones. It is to cultural attitudes to and images of wolves that this book now turns.

2 Lupophobia

In Angela Carter's short story 'The Company of Wolves', the narrator warns readers to 'Fear and flee the wolf; for, worst of all, the wolf may be more than he seems.'[1] For centuries, peoples whose lives have been crossed by wolves have worried about that 'more than he seems'. Part of the fear might be that evoked by a large carnivore but it is often more than this. It is also the fear of what lurks within the wolf and drives it to behave in the ways that it is imagined to behave, and people have sought to protect themselves against this wolf in all its forms.

For several thousand years early humans and wolves were hunters and scavengers of the wild animals that were freely available to both of them. The problem of the wolf for humans, and perhaps of humans for the wolf, began between 10,000 and 6,000 years ago with the domestication of sheep and goats, creatures with which the lives of wolves were to be forever entangled, whether they actually lived in close proximity to them or not. With domestication a new class of animals emerged that was not the result of neutral processes of evolution but rather a combination of natural and cultural processes, shaped and maintained for specifically human purposes. Two of the complex relationships between humans and animals in the context of domestication are important here: mutual dependency and ownership. Domesticated animals came to be dependent

Francisco Goya, 'Esto es lo peor!' (This is the worst!), from the series *The Disasters of War*, 1810–20, etching. Goya depicts a cunning, dangerous wild animal (perhaps representing the government), assisted by a friar, writing an official document.

on humans for food, water and their general welfare and humans came to depend on them as part of their strategies for subsistence and general provisioning. These animals also became the property of those committed to a relationship of care and control over them. Their owners therefore made an investment in these animals, which entered into their economies and so into their social and cultural worlds. As property they became subject to risk and challenge from others who might seek to take possession of them. They were in danger of being taken by other humans or through predation by wild carnivores, both of which were often perceived as theft. Once animals were in their care, those who lived by pastoralism began to fear and revile wolves for both they and their flocks became vulnerable to their predations. Wolves became unwanted, often feared, intruders into human affairs.

Exceptions to the fear and vulnerability expressed by pastoralists whose flocks are threatened by wolves are nomadic herders. Although herders must be vigilant against wolf attacks, the wolf is often represented in such societies as a worthy rival. Nomadic herders, such as those of Mongolia or the reindeer herders of circum-polar regions, and their animals live in the same spaces as wild predators, since such societies have scarcely any domesticated pasture or fields into which wolves can symbolically intrude. Both groups are struggling for survival and people know that their animals are likely to be targets for predators. The herds might be vulnerable but the herdsmen do not seem to see themselves as victims: wolves are regarded as simply doing something natural. In such cultures there is often a strong sense of the need for self-reliance and for accepting and overcoming physical hardship. This translates into the need for people to confront wolves, do battle with them, attack them and kill them when they can. In such places and cultures wolves are simply part of the harsh environment and realities of the world.[2]

'The Wolf', illustration depicting a shepherd defending his flock from a wolf, *Illustrated Times* (1862).

'Iskander and the Wolf', from the *Shahnama* of Ferdowsi (The Book of Kings), C. AD 977–1010.

Playing on the everyday, local concerns of the settled shepherding world of ancient Greece, Aesop (sixth to fifth centuries BC) created a series of moralizing stories featuring wolves. Perhaps the most famous concerns the shepherd who abused the trust of his fellow villagers by shouting that wolves were attacking his flocks when there was no such danger. He enjoyed the alarm he caused as they rushed to his aid. Several times the shepherd had fun at their expense but he was suitably punished when wolves really did attack, the villagers no longer responded to his cries, and his sheep were eaten. The moral of 'Crying "Wolf!"' is directed against those who knowingly raise false alarms, but importantly here it is the image of wolves approaching a flock of sheep that constitutes a generic picture of danger.

Other tales of wolves in Aesop depend on understanding the need to maintain the proper relationships between the shepherd and the dogs that help guard the sheep. Here Aesop taps into the anxiety that many have expressed about the possible close affinity between the trusted domesticated dog and the wild wolf from which it is thought to descend, to which it might be dangerously closely related and to which it might revert. The fear is that the power of original wildness could destabilize the fragility of domestication. In one tale wolves approach a group of sheepdogs and claim that they should not attack them for they are brothers under the skin. The wolves mock the dogs for becoming slaves to men, for suffering beatings and having to wear collars, with their only reward being the scraps of food their masters do not want. They suggest that the dogs should let them kill the sheep and they would share the spoils. The dogs commit the most treacherous act for sheepdogs and let the wolves into the sheepfold. But before they attack the sheep, the wolves kill all the dogs.

In other Aesopian tales naive shepherds treat apparently meek wolves as though they are no different from domestic dogs. They

'The Shepherd and the Wolf', from *The Medici Aesop*, 15th century.

39

raise wolf cubs with their sheepdogs, hoping to tame them and
train them to guard their flocks, only for the wolves to reveal their
true nature and attack the sheep. A particularly gullible shepherd
commits the act of ultimate folly. He believes that a meek wolf
that follows his flock is acting as a protector rather than a predator and leaves his animals in its care. As soon as he leaves the
wolf kills most of them. In the end the shepherds suffer for fail-
ing to recognize that such wolves are dissimulating in order to
achieve their wild ends of turning sheep into food, something
that sheepdogs must be trusted never to do.

Aesop was not writing a natural history of animals in the
Greek world, but rather was using animals to warn, criticize and
moralize about human behaviour. Through repetition across the
centuries, his wolf tales have added to the wolf's image as a particularly dangerous enemy of humankind, to be feared precisely
because it uses guile to slip into the human world.

Such fears are also voiced in the Old Testament, where part
of Isaiah's vision of a messianic, utopian future involves the ending of predation of wild animals on domestic beasts. It is a
vision that specifically links the wolf and the lamb in peaceful
co-existence, with all other previously fierce creatures becoming
so meek that a mere child would be able to control them:

40

The wolf also shall dwell with the lamb, and the leopard shall lie down with the kid; and the calf and the young lion and the fatling together; and a little child shall lead them.[3]

The image is powerfully evocative because the idea of wolves dwelling with lambs without harming them would have been

Gustave Doré, 'The Wolf turned Shepherd', illustration of an Aesop fable, 19th century.

Amen, amen, I say to you: He that entereth not by the door into the sheepfold, but climbeth up another way, the same is a thief and a robber.

But he that entereth in by the door is the shepherd of the sheep.

Cath

unimaginable for pastoralists of the time. So too would a later development of this harmless proximity when 'The wolf and the lamb shall feed together'.[4] Not only will the wolf not prey on the lamb but, as later in the same verse, 'the lion shall eat straw like the bullock': it will become a herbivore and never need to kill again. For such a relationship between sheep and wolves to develop, the world would have to turn upside down, but until then people had to be vigilant against the wolf – an animal, and image of an animal, used in the New Testament to warn early Christians of other dangers to their well-being.

Much of the symbolism of Jesus and his followers derives from a pastoral economy and culture in which sheep are both valuable and vulnerable. The people to whom Jesus preached would have been aware of the dangers that real wolves posed to shepherds, making the wolf an ideal creature as a warning of the moral, religious and physical dangers that confronted his followers. Jesus explains his relationship with his followers as being like that of a true shepherd, ever vigilant and protective of his flock:

> I am the good shepherd: the good shepherd giveth his life for the sheep.
>   But he that is an hireling, and not the true shepherd, whose own the sheep are not, seeth the wolf coming, and leaveth the sheep, and fleeth: and the wolf catcheth them, and scattereth the sheep.[5]

Jesus also sends his followers out into the world 'as sheep in the midst of wolves'[6] or, with even more vulnerability, 'as lambs among wolves'.[7] Here the image is a naturalistic one. Just as sheep that wander away from the shepherd and the flock into the wilderness are in danger of being eaten by wolves, so his followers, leaving the safety of their community, are in danger of attack by their enemies – as of course is Jesus in his representational form of the Lamb of God. However, there is an important shift in Jesus' development of the image and character of the

GALLAHER'S CIGARETTES.

THE WOLF IN SHEEPS CLOTHING.

COPYRIGHT

'The Wolf in Sheep's Clothing', Gallaher's cigarette card, 1922.

wolf in his warning of 'false prophets' who would come 'in sheep's clothing, but inwardly they are ravening wolves'.[8] Rather than a naturalistic image, in which the shepherd protects his flock against hungry wolves, this is a moralistic one that requires the attribution of duplicity to a wild animal that becomes a man-animal.

There are two parts to this image: the manner of approach of the predatory wolf and its character. The first part is rather peculiar. The suggestion that wolves disguise themselves in order to get among their prey is certainly not a naturalistic image drawn from encounters with wolves, but it works extremely well with the fearful idea that the outer form of a docile, unthreatening sheep hides a predator within. Jesus doubles the fearful image by emphasizing the wolf's dangerous appetite. Here the wolf does not have a natural hunger that drives it to kill and eat as all carnivores must. It has a 'ravening' character, suggesting an excessive, unnatural, unacceptable and immoral behaviour and appetite. Wolves do wrong by attacking sheep, but their supposed motivation – ravening rather than simply ravenous – is more disturbing than simply harmful predation. Wolves become perceived and represented as creatures of dangerous and wicked intention because humans need an image for their own wickedness and wrongdoing. Thus wicked people who attack others are like wolves and the essential wickedness of the wolf is more firmly established, and played back onto the wolf, by being imagined as similar to such people. Jesus' comparison between wolves and dangerously treacherous people is thus an important development in the imagined character of the wolf. It offers a legitimacy for centuries of wolf killing. Wolves were not killed simply because their attacks resulted in economic losses. They were

Anon., 'The Wolf in Sheep's Clothing', 1818, engraving.

persecuted because they were perceived to be evil-intentioned, criminal animals.

The pastoral world of sheep, shepherds and wolves is also the context for the earliest stories of human-wolf metamorphoses as a form of punishment. In the Babylonian epic *Gilgamesh*, one of the world's oldest literary texts (written and compiled in different forms between 2100 and 1200 BC), Gilgamesh, rejecting an offer of marriage from Ištar, goddess of sex and war, reminds her about her harsh treatment of previous lovers:

> You loved the shepherd, the grazier, the herdsman,
>   who regularly piled up for you [bread baked in] embers,
>   slaughtering kids for you everyday.
> You struck him and turned him into a wolf,
>   so his own shepherd boys drive him away,
>   and his dogs take bites at his thighs.[9]

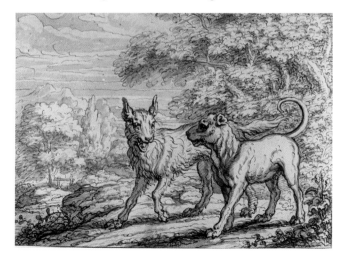

Francis Barlow, (*c.* 1626–1704), illustration of fable XCVII, 'The Wolf and the Dog', from Aesop's Fables.

Ištar's manner of casting away this rejected lover is speci-fically destructive. The shepherd is transformed into the very animal that flocks must be protected against and is pursued as wolves should be pursued. The awfulness of the punishment is not simply that the man has become an animal but that he has become a wolf, his own worst enemy, and a creature that the whole of his world must turn against. With sheepdogs, his trained companions and agents of protection, snapping at him, and with his fellow shepherds in pursuit, the shepherd/wolf is forced out into the wilderness. Although the shepherd has com-mitted no crime against his fellow men, and his transformation is imposed on him, as a wolf he cannot remain with them and must be driven away into the proper domain of wolves.

The second example is the Greco-Roman story of the trans-formation, by an angry Zeus, of the mythical King Lycaon, a name already suggestive of someone wolfish (the Greek for wolf being *lykos*). Not all of the different versions of why Zeus was angered by the king result in him becoming a wolf, but in those that do the central issue seems to have been the offer of an unnatural meal. Zeus visits the palace of Lycaon in disguise and is offered, either by Lycaon himself or by his sons, a meal consisting of human meat (there are various versions of who formed the basis of this meal).[10] As punishment for being party to murder, for converting human flesh into food and for attempting to trick a god into cannibalism, Zeus turns Lycaon into a wolf who must live by killing the flocks that his shepherds attempt to defend:

> He fled in fear and reached the silent fields
> And howled his heart out, trying in vain to speak.
> With rabid mouth he turned his lust for slaughter
> Against the flocks, delighting still in blood.
> His clothes changed to coarse hair, his arms to legs –

He was a wolf, yet kept some human trace,
The same grey hair, the same fierce face, the same
Wild eyes, the same image of savagery.[11]

A wolf in sheep's clothing offers an image of a creature of dangerous intent disguised, but this is only superficial and the wolf within can be revealed by recognizing or removing the disguise. Here the wolf does not transform itself into a sheep but merely takes its skin as a cloak.

A much more disturbing image of the wolf being more than it seems comes with tales of the ability of people to turn themselves into wolves in order to prey on their fellow humans. The possibility of a werewolf living among normal people provokes fear because of the chance that such a threat lurks within an apparently normal human form and dwells within society. The werewolf is a profoundly troubling creature created through essential boundary transgressions: between the human and the animal, the civilized and the bestial, the domesticated and the wild. Whereas the wolf can be separated from its sheep's clothing, for both exist independently of the other, this cannot be done with the werewolf, which is both human and wolf at the same time, even though its outward appearance changes. Although there is always a double transformation with the werewolf – the human becomes wolf and then reverts to being human – the direction of that transformation is significant. Werewolves are not wolves able to take on human form and then return to being wolves, they are always humans who metamorphose. Werewolves begin as humans who are able to attack people because they have become dangerous wild animals. The concern, then, is with people who are able to take on the supposed ravening spirit and ferocious killing power of the wolf. Although the werewolf has often been described as half man and half beast, it is really a more disturbing creature in which human and wolf become conjoined to create a monstrous beast that exceeds both. This is frightening because, in either incarnation, there is always a different creature hidden within.

Although a monster, the werewolf did not develop from a mythical or imaginary creature. It was the real wolf, and all that it was imagined to be, that formed the animal part of the werewolf. In the landscapes and times in which werewolves emerged there were other carnivores – bears, lynxes, foxes, dogs – that could have conjoined with the human. However, it was only the wolf that possessed a long cultural history of the necessary fearsome qualities to make it a creature more dangerous than any other. For Montague Summers, the noted early twentieth-century writer on the occult, the distinctive features of the wolf that made it so dangerous were its:

> unbridled cruelty, bestial ferocity, and ravening hunger. His strength, his cunning, his speed were regarded as abnormal, almost eerie qualities, he had something of the demon, of hell. His is the symbol of Night and Winter, of Stress and Storm, the dark and mysterious harbinger of Death.[12]

Summers also pointed out that the wolf, as the predator of defenceless lambs, was the eternal enemy of the Lamb of God. That the wolf had 'ever been the inevitable, remorseless enemy of man' made it appalling that a person would seek to merge with such a creature.

The first literary description of a human voluntarily changing into a wolf is in Virgil's *Eclogues*, in which Alphesiboeus recounts how:

Moeris himself has given these herbs as poisons harvested for me in Pontus. Many such are produced in Pontus. There have I seen Moeris become a wolf by using these and hide himself away in the woods and seen him arouse souls from the depths of tombs.[13]

Unlike the human punished by becoming a wolf, here the human as wolf takes on darker connotations. Not only does Moeris seemingly wish to become a wolf, he has the magical means to become one and commit the horrific act of violating the sanctity of the dead in their tombs. There is a relationship here between the poetic and the real: not only were wolves accused for their natural predations on livestock, they were also commonly blamed for unnatural predation on human bodies by opening recently dug graves and scavenging the corpses of soldiers on battlefields, a lupine crime that fed back into representations of the unnatural behaviour of werewolves.

One particular representation of the werewolf in Latin literature is important for its introduction of a significant theme of werewolfery: the transformation of the wolfly creature back into human form and the recognition by others that the person not only has been a wolf but *is* a werewolf. In Petronius' *Satyricon*, Niceros recounts his encounter with a werewolf and how he observed the transformation from human to wolf.

Niceros, a slave, decides to visit Melissa, with whom he is in love. He persuades a soldier lodging in his master's house to accompany him on the journey. They make an early start, with the moon shining brightly, and their path takes them past a graveyard where the soldier wanders among the tombs. Niceros notices that his companion has stripped off his clothes, laid them in a heap and urinated around them. The clothes turn to stone and the man into a wolf that runs, howling, into the forest. Niceros

races to Melissa's house, where she tells him that a wolf has attacked their cattle but they have driven it off and one of the labourers has managed to wound it in the neck. On his return journey Niceros finds that the stone clothes are gone and in their place there is a pool of blood. At home he finds the soldier in bed being attended to by a doctor for a large wound in his neck. Niceros immediately recognizes him as a werewolf.

Here clothes are highly significant in terms of the processes of transformation. The shedding of clothes, markers of civilization, is essential for the movement towards the animal and their recovery equally essential for the return to human form. This shedding of one form of covering to allow another to emerge is also picked up in the popular belief that werewolves, in human form, were marked by having hair growing inside their bodies. If the wolfish hair is inside, then a turning inside out, in either direction, reveals a different creature: a human with a wolf inside or a wolf with a human inside. It is worth noting here that the Latin term for werewolf, *versipellis*, meaning to change skin, captures this sense of different surfaces relating to, or revealing and obscuring, different identities.

The new element in this story is that the injury done to the wolf is carried back through the transformation and is marked on the human body; it is this that reveals to others that the person is a werewolf. As will be shown later, this could have dire consequences, often execution or some other form of death, for the person so revealed. In the case of the soldier werewolf there was no such dramatic ending. Niceros merely avoids him at mealtimes: 'I realized he was a werewolf and afterwards I couldn't have taken a bite of bread in his company, not if you killed me for it' is his final comment in the story.[14] The concern here, as with many early cases of werewolfery, seems to be with the unnatural transformation rather than what the manwolf does. Just as

Lycaon in wolf form attacks cattle, so does the soldier in this story – perfectly normal wolf behaviour. There is no sense that the soldier should be punished for his ability to transform himself and he seems to be able to return to civilized society when he resumes human form.

In these early accounts of transformations there seems to be little concern with the werewolf as a creature of evil. It was in northern continental Europe in the Middle Ages that a more profound anxiety emerged about the nature of the werewolf because of its unnatural predation on humans. By then the biblical wolf, symbolic of the human threat to the spiritual lives of early Christians, had become a creature inspired by, or in league with, Satan and was now perceived to be a diabolical danger both spiritually and physically. Werewolves were thus swept up in the general concern with witchcraft and the work of Satan. Theologians debated the nature of werewolfery and both Church and State authorities sought out werewolves, as they did witches, and punished them. The popular fear of werewolfery was based on the potential and actual attacks by large numbers of wolves across much of Europe. The ordinary, if sometimes severe, predation by wolves on livestock or the less common attacks on humans could be dealt with by hunting them. However, when it was felt that such attacks were of particular ferocity, or did not fit into expectations of natural wolf behaviour, then the werewolf was there as a possible explanation.

In a study of wolf attacks and the trials of werewolves in sixteenth- and seventeenth-century Burgundy, Caroline Oates identifies key themes in the nature of such attacks and in the metamorphoses of werewolves.[15] The primary fear was that of a wolf attacking people, but occasionally there was something particular that caused people to think that the wolf was rather more than a natural wolf. She suggests that there were three

stages in the process by which a wolf attack became treated as a werewolf attack. The process began with an encounter with a wolf or wolves in which those attacked or who witnessed attacks saw, or remembered, something suspicious about the animal – perhaps its unnaturally large size, unusual ferocity or some physical deformity.

The next stage involved some sign or circumstantial evidence for an individual to be suspected of being a werewolf, such as a wolf attack occurring shortly before or after a person had dealings with a suspected witch, an unexplained absence at the time of a wolf attack, or the discovery of someone in the forest as the hunters suddenly lost track of a previously seen wolf. All these signs could lead to suspicions of the presence of a werewolf. But just as a wolf with unusual features could raise suspicions, so too could a person with unusual features or

54

abnormalities. Werewolves were also exposed when, as in Petronius' tale, a person was discovered to be suffering from the injuries inflicted on a wolf. Oates explores several such accounts including the following:

A hunter from the region of Poligny saw a wolf one day and shot it with an arrow. Following the trail of blood, he traced the wolf to a house, where he discovered a woman tending an injured man, who was wounded in precisely the same part of the body as the wolf had been. The hunter informed the magistrate at Poligny, who had the man arrested and tortured until the truth was known. The suspect confessed that, using a certain ointment made by demonic arts, he had assumed the form of a wolf.[16]

The final stage of treating a wolf attack as a werewolf attack required a general belief in the existence of such creatures. The witnesses to unusual wolf attacks and the accusers and accused in these cases believed that people could effect such metamorphoses and could explain how they were brought about. Such transformations were not accidental or natural, and they were certainly not unmotivated. There was no sense that these people were victims of their condition and there was no pity for them. Such transformations were always intended to do harm – sometimes to attack animals but sometimes, more worryingly, to cause harm to people in a more frightening and effective way than could be achieved in human form. Perhaps the most frightening aspect of such attacks was that humans killed by a werewolf could be eaten by the creature, a fate the victims of most common murderers did not suffer. An attack by a natural wolf was both frightening and shocking – humans should not become the food of wild animals – but at least it was simply a natural attack by a natural predator. A werewolf attack was of a different order. It was an attack by a human, albeit in wolf form, and so the devouring of the victim was an act of cannibalism.

One of the most gruesome individual histories of werewolf transformations and predations is the late sixteenth-century account of the life and death of Peter Stumpf of Bedburg, a small town near Cologne. According to contemporary reports, Stumpf was inclined to evil from a young age and was soon supported in his desires and practices by the Devil who:

> gave him a girdle which, being put around him, he was transformed into the likeness of a greedy, devouring wolf, strong and mighty, with eyes great and large, which in the night sparkled like brands of fire; a mouth great and wide, with the most sharp and cruel teeth; a huge body and mighty paws. And no sooner should he put off the same girdle, but presently he should appear in his former shape, according to the proportion of a man, as if he had never been changed.[17]

If a person displeased Stumpf he would attack, kill and eat them while in his wolf form. He would also rape women, although it is not clear whether in the shape of a man or wolf, and then kill them. Not content with preying on local people, he also committed incest with his daughter. His wife was a witch and he even took his son into the woods, where he transformed himself into a wolf and then 'most cruelly slew him, which done he presently ate the brains out of his head as a most savory and dainty means to staunch his greedy appetite'.[18]

Stumpf's reign of terror was brought to an end during a wolf hunt. As mastiffs closed in, the wolfish Stumpf became a man again. The hunters who had witnessed this metamorphosis were unsure whether this was a man or 'some Devil in a man's likeness'. He was identified and handed over to the local magistrates. Tortured on the rack, he confessed to his crimes and to being a werewolf. His wife and daughter were also tried and condemned. They were burned to death but Stumpf's end was more elaborate. He was tied to a wheel, red-hot pincers were used to pull off his flesh and his arms and legs were broken. His head was cut off and his body was burned. After the execution a tall pole was erected in a public place; mounted on this was the wheel on which he had been broken, and above it was placed a wooden carving of a wolf, 'to show unto all men the shape wherein he executed those cruelties'. Above all of this was placed the head of Stumpf himself.[19]

The carved wolf is, in association with the head of Stumpf, a representation of both criminality and evil; a display advertising that the criminal has been dealt with and others are likely to

'Of the Wolf', illustration from Edward Topsell, *The History of Four-footed Beasts and Serpents* (1658).

57

meet that same end. Wolves killed by human hunters were later displayed in public places to demonstrate that criminal animals had been duly and rightly punished.

With the gradual eradication of wolves across Europe the fear that some attacks were actually by werewolves seemed to recede. Werewolves only re-emerged when a real fear of humans taking animal form had long disappeared. Brian Frost, in his comprehensive study of werewolf literature, which includes reference to some 900 works of popular fiction (poems, short stories, magazine stories and novels), suggests that the werewolf in literature wanes from the medieval period and only emerges again in the early nineteenth century.[20] The first novel that features a werewolf as its main character was George W. M. Reynolds's *Wagner, the Wehr-Wolf*, serialized in magazine form between 1846 and 1847. Two major French literary figures, Alexandre Dumas *père* and Guy de Maupassant, contributed to the genre with, respectively, *The Wolf-Leader* (1857) and 'The Wolf' (1884). At a time when there were few wolves to pose any danger to humans and when werewolves slipped into the realm of myth and superstition, literary werewolves could now thrill, frighten and fascinate a largely urban population. The werewolves created in the nineteenth and twentieth centuries were not, in the main, very different from their medieval counterparts and they often prowled through pseudo-medieval rural settings of dark forests, craggy wilderness and sinister castles. A few suffered from involuntary and unwished-for transformations – the curse of the werewolf or lycanthropy – that had tragic consequences for their human relationships. Many were in league with the Devil, through whose power they effected their transformations. Others suffered a transformation because they were psychologically unable to repress the beast that lurks, potentially, inside every civilized person. All of them used their wolf form to do what werewolves had been doing for centuries – viciously attack and kill innocent people and then, sometimes, feed on them. But there was something different about these creatures. As Frost points out, a new breed of werewolves came about in the modern period, 'the werewolf who stalked his victims among the streets and alleys of modern cities'.[21] Earlier werewolf attacks took place in the countryside, the natural habitat of wolves. Cities, the space of human habitation and civilization, were not places where dangerous animals should roam and threaten humans. This made urban werewolf attacks particularly threatening and problematic for the characters in the stories. It also made them thrilling for those who read them.

The nature of the transformation into wolf form was always a matter of concern in the early reports of werewolfery. For Christian theologians these creatures posed questions relating to the immutability, or otherwise, of human and animal forms or whether such transformations were only apparent – illusions caused by the Devil and his demons. For the non-theologically minded such niceties were of less concern than who became werewolves and what they did once transformed. There was, however, little lingering over the process of transformation itself in reports of werewolfery. Instead, a human simply became a beast through a variety of means. It was only when the danger of attack by humans in wolf form was safely in the past, and regarded as an irrational belief of a primitive mentality, that a different public could enjoy the process of a person becoming a monster. When werewolves re-emerged in popular fiction in the nineteenth century writers began to describe in graphic detail the metamorphosis of the human and this became part of the thrill or horror of the weird and the grotesque. Reynolds's *Wagner, the Wehr-Wolf* is a fine example of such sensationalist writing:

But lo! What awful change is taking place in the form of that doomed being? His handsome countenance elongates into one of a savage and brute-like shape – the rich garment which he wears becomes a rough, shaggy, and wiry skin; his body loses its human contours . . . and with a rush like a hurling wind, the wretch starts wildly away – no longer a man, but a monstrous wolf![22]

Illustration for a story of a German hunter in America who falls into a wolf den, 1847, engraving.

It was cinema that offered new possibilities for revelling in the horror, fear and agony of the actual transformation into a dangerous wild beast or, later, for witnessing the beast breaking out from within the human. The subject's celluloid debut came in *The Werewolf* (1913), which featured a Navajo woman who, in wolf form, attacked invading white people, rather than the more usual transformation of a man into a wild animal. Hollywood's long interest in the horror potential of the now familiar werewolf began with *The Werewolf of London* (1935), which features a scientist who is bitten by a wild animal while on a botanical trip to Tibet. He contracts lycanthropy and, back in London, begins to develop a dual life of civilized man by day and murdering wolf by night. The image of the werewolf is little developed in the film but six years later the same studio, Universal, offered the public the first visual transformation of man into werewolf. *The Wolf Man* (1941) tells the story of Larry Talbot, played by Lon Chaney Jr, who transforms into a murderous wolf every full moon after being bitten by a werewolf while trying to save a woman from an attack. He is finally killed by his own father who beats him with a walking stick with a silver wolf head handle; in death he returns once more to human form. A huge amount of effort went into making the transformation spectacular, but the special effects of the time were limited to photographing the actor's face, adding a layer of yak hair, photographing it again and continuing the process until the effect was achieved. The dissolve from Larry Talbot to the wolfman takes only a few seconds but it took many hours in the make-up room. It would seem that the producers thought the transformation was the exciting element of the film and there was little attempt to develop a complex plot, to frighten the audience or to interest them in the plight of werewolves. The *New York Times Review* commented on its release:

> Most of the budget was spent on Mr Chaney's face, which is rather terrifying, resembling as it does a sort of Mr Hyde badly in need of a shave . . . nobody is going to go on believing in werewolves . . . if the custodians of these legends don't tell them with a more convincing imaginative touch.[23]

Makers of werewolf films were later able to employ increasingly sophisticated special effects to make the essential transformation from human to wolf more convincing and imaginative and thus horrific. The skill required in rendering the emergence of a monster was recognized when the first Academy Award for Best Make-up was won by Rick Baker for the human-to-wolf transformation in *An American Werewolf in London* (1981).

Perhaps the film industry took heed of the anonymous critic cited above, because *The Wolf Man* marks the beginning of the werewolf's cinema popularity. In turn cinema became both a custodian and a creator of werewolf legends and images. In the 1940s thirteen werewolf films were made, though only six in the 1950s, but then came a steady rise: in the 1960s (25), 1970s (38), 1980s (51), 1990s (47) and, since 2000, 67. The enduring power of the metamorphosis of a person into a wolf as the basis for telling a story about the human condition is perhaps revealed by the fact that the recent *The Wolfman*, released in early 2010, is a

remake of the first full-length werewolf film, *The Werewolf of London* from 1935.

As well as creating more credibly wolf-like werewolves, cinema (and this is also found in twentieth-century literature) added something new to the earlier causes of werewolfery – the transmission of the condition from werewolf to human through contamination from a bite. In earlier stories, the werewolf was exposed through injuries to a wolf that remained present when it regained human form. In the twentieth century, however, the injuries inflicted by a werewolf became the means by which werewolves are able to reproduce – they breed through infection. Early werewolves always began with, and emerged from, the human but what was created in the twentieth century was a condition that began with the animal, with werewolves as a species that could transform humans into animals. As a result the person infected with the condition, usually through a bite, or who inherits it as a curse, does not revel in the power to do evil but rather suffers guilt and feels remorse when in human form. Kim Newman, a noted analyst of the horror genre, comments that, 'it's a quirk that werewolf movies should predominantly deal with sympathetic, semi-tragic monsters rather than the wicked werewolves found in folklore'.[24]

Of the many stories, in the genres of folk or fairy tales, of wolves as threatening to humans, one has had more influence than any other in creating the image of wolves as bad creatures. Since the earliest written version by Charles Perrault in 1697, the tale of Little Red Riding Hood has been retold, rewritten and re-invented. Each retelling has added to the bad reputation of wolves. For the Little Red Riding Hood story to work as a morality tale it needed a villain, and the feared and hated wolf was ideal. The wolf's general reputation brought it into the story and, once the creature was trapped there, its wide popularity ensured that this representation of wolfish behaviour became fundamental in shaping views of wolves.

Although essentially concerned with what little girls should or should not do, the dangers of what lurks outside the domain of civilization and the threat of the wild intruding into human spaces and relations, the stories are certainly not based on what wolves might do when encountering a solitary and defenceless person. This is a very un-wolf-like wolf. It does not do what a hungry wolf might do – pounce on her and eat her on the spot. Nor does it seek to find out where the girl's grandmother might be so that it may have two meals.

The wolf in these tales can be read as anthropomorphized, but a more complex and disturbing reading of the nature of the wolf is possible. A clue to what sort of creature this might be is to be found in what Jack Zipes argues are the remnants of the original oral stories.[25] Here the girl does not encounter a *loup*, a wolf, but a *bzou*, a werewolf – a heady mixture of animal ferocity

Metamorphosis. Still from *An American Werewolf in London* (1981).

65

LITTLE RED RIDING HOOD, on the way to her grandmother, meets a big wolf, who says, "GOOD-MORNING," and "WHERE ARE YOU GOING?" After hearing, where she was going, the wolf ran away.

1753

From Georgie

and appetites and human passions and desires – and the wolf of these stories has transformative aspects of the werewolf about it.

The wolf has the power of human speech and the girl seems unable to recognize it as a potentially wild animal when she talks to it in the forest. Later the wolf is able to disguise its animal voice and persuade the grandmother, by imitating the girl's voice, to open the door to her house. In the crucial scene before it attacks the girl, it becomes a wolf in human clothing dressed as the grandmother. Once again, Red Riding Hood is unable to recognize the dangerous wild animal although she does think her grandmother seems different. In some versions she sees through the disguise and escapes; in most the wolf devours her

Anon., Little Red Riding Hood encounters the speaking wolf, 1906.

Ceci vous prouve, fillette,
Que souvent le loup vous guette
Et qu'il croque les enfants
Qui sont désobéissants.

The moral of Red Riding Hood: 'This shows, little girl, that often the wolf is lying in wait for you, and he bites disobedient children', c. 1900, postcard.

as it admits what its teeth are for, 'the better to eat you'. Where the wolf attempts to attack Red Riding Hood is highly significant. Instead of pouncing on the girl as she enters the house, it lures her into the bedroom and she is persuaded to get into bed with the wolf. In some versions she is persuaded to undress and burn her clothes – a fraught combination of a naked girl and a clothed wild animal. Here there is an intention to devour but the devouring always takes place in bed; clearly this desire is sexual as much as nutritional.

The wolf has gone beyond a wild animal that might kill and eat people. The wolf that was feared as rapacious in terms of appetite now becomes a potential rapist, a lustful creature with a sexual appetite. In modern parlance it is akin to a sexual stalker who grooms a girl with friendly talk before it attempts to make her its victim. This characterization of the wolf was clearly not drawn from what natural wolves do but rather emerges from a concern for what men are or what they might become. It is the wolf, rather than any other existing wild animal, however, that

"I wouldn't let you eat *my* grandmother!"

becomes the victim of human imagination. This image of the predatory wolf becomes yet another cultural layer of how people imagined and feared wolves. Echoes of this sexualized wolf can still be heard in the French expression '*voir le loup*' (to see the wolf), referring to a young woman losing her virginity, and more faintly in the 'wolf whistle' that sometimes follows a woman along a street.

Both wolves in sheep's clothing and werewolves operate as lone wolves rather than as pack animals. However, the image of a pack approaching and attacking its prey, based in part on naturalistic ideas about wolves, has also created the fearsome representation of wolf attacks on humans. A necessary and efficient means of hunting for a wolf pack in the natural world, with several animals attempting to bring down their prey, becomes rendered in the world of the imagination as a ferocious and merciless assault, coordinated by brutal and vicious predators. It is the image of the wolf pack as a determined and coordinated group of killer animals that becomes a frightening possibility when directed against people. The horror here is of humans pursued and hunted in an open and deliberate way by wild animals that seem to have no fear of them. The fear of such attacks is usually set in the cultural context of the potential dangers awaiting in the untamed wilderness of forests. As Aleksander Pluskowski has explored in depth, 'One of the most evocative associations in the European popular imagination is the relationship between the wolf and the woods', especially 'the dramatic, haunted and always dark woods'.[26] That relationship is not a problem if the wolf stays in its proper, natural space and people remain in theirs. The fear only begins when wolves come out of the woods or when people venture into them. In either crossing of boundaries there is fear and the potential danger of an encounter.

The wolf as sexual predator – a 'wolf whistle' toy.

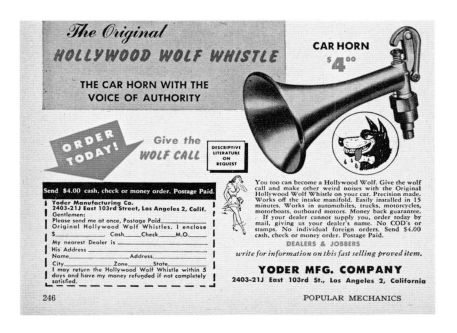

The most dramatic versions in both literature and art of such fears are connected with travellers having to journey (often in winter to add to the bleak atmosphere) through inhospitable mountains, steppes or forests. The eerie and sinister howling of wolves is heard in the distance, the horses pulling the carriage or sleigh are made to increase their pace, the howling comes closer, the travellers realize they are being followed, hunted. Dark shapes are seen closing in; vicious, burning, yellow eyes are glimpsed; an attack is imminent. When the wolves attack they do so as a ferocious pack that attempts to encircle the travellers, snapping and lungeing at the horses and humans. Often people fall and are killed mercilessly; others shoot at the wolves or slash at them with whatever weapons they have to repel the attack. A report in

Advertisement for the 'Hollywood Wolf Whistle' car horn, 1948.

the *New York Times* in 1911 describes an extraordinary wolf attack on a wedding party in eastern Russia in just these terms. Even the bride and groom were deliberately thrown from their sledge 'to meet a horrible fate' by those desperate to survive. Although purportedly describing 'a ghastly reality surpass[ing] almost anything ever imagined by a fiction writer', the report can perhaps be better interpreted as a description of the fears of wolf attacks at their most nightmarish and monstrous.[27]

Aleksander Pluskowski comments: 'In identifying with wild animals such as wolves . . . either personally or through a deity, warriors effectively converted themselves into ruthless predators and their enemies into natural prey.'[28] A northern example of the association of a deity with warriors and wolves is Odin, the god of death in battle, who is often accompanied by two wolves, Geri and Freki (the names mean Greed or Voracity). While Odin takes the souls of the warriors slain in battle to Valhalla their

Bad fortune deterred – keeping the wolf from the door, 1911, postcard.

Prosperity attends you
You never seem to fail:
And if the wolf came to your door
He'd surely turn his tail.

John Martin
(1789–1854),
a warrior defends
his wife and
children from
a pack of wolves,
drawing on paper.

earthly remains are eaten by Geri and Freki. Odin was also depicted with a human wolf warrior at his side.

There is a long European history of wolf warriors, both in the sense of warriors being likened to a ferocious pack of wolves when in battle and in warrior self-identification with wolves and using wolfskins and wolf images as part of their battle dress. The *Iliad* offers a comparison of wolves and warriors in the description of the Danaans attacking the Trojan lines:

> As ravenous wolves come down on lambs and kids
> Astray from some flock that in hilly country
> Splits in two by a shepherd's negligence,
> And quickly wolves bear off the defenceless things.[29]

Anon., Russian travellers defending themselves against wolves, c. 19th century.

Although Germanic warriors identified with a range of animals, including the bear, marten, boar and horse, it was the wolf that seems to have had the greatest allure as a totemic animal in terms of developing a warrior style. Roman armies also marched with soldiers bearing wolf standards and shields or dressed in wolfskins. It has been suggested that Germanic wolf warriors, clad in wolfskins, can be discerned on Trajan's Column, built to celebrate victory over the Dacians (AD 101–106).[30]

Not only did people drape themselves with wolf parts but they also took wolf names. Many kings and warriors recorded in Anglo-Saxon texts had *wulf* as a prefix or suffix in their names – Wulfhere, Cynewulf, Ceonwulf, Wulfheard, Eanwulf, Wulfmeer, Wulfstan and Aethelwulf – perhaps indicating an appropriation of a wolf quality to their person. But the ferocious wolf image

74

could equally be played onto their enemies, as in the poem of the 'Battle of Maldon' (AD 991), where the raiding Vikings are called 'slaughterous wolves' or 'war wolves'. Speidel also notes that wolf names were common among pre-Christian Germanic warriors: Wolfhroc (Wolf-Frock), Wolfhetan (Wolf Hide), Isangrim (Grey Mask), Scrutolf (Garb Wolf), Wolfgang (Wolf Gait) and Wolf-dregil (Wolf Runner).

Centuries later, wolf warriors re-emerged in Germany. The twentieth century provides a striking example of the linking of wolves, hunting and human warfare: the German U-boats referred to as wolf packs in the Second World War. In 1941 Admiral Karl Dönitz developed new tactics in submarine warfare. The official term for the tactics was *Gruppen* (group), as in *Gruppentaktik*, but a wolfish term was commonly used for these groups of submarines. That term was *rudel*, meaning pack, and normally used for packs of wolves or dogs. The power of the image was that of collective and collaborative hunting and attack. The hunting involved searching for prey by stealth, silently prowling the seascapes in search of victims and closing in undetected. Each submarine patrolled separately, but when an individual commander located enemy shipping he did not launch a lone attack. Instead he shadowed the convoy, radioed battle command at home and, if possible, made contact with other boats. Members of the group, thus alerted, came together swiftly to mount an attack. Here the hunting pack in pursuit of their prey cooperated in the attack of a defensive herd, attempting to get in among them, create panic and kill the most vulnerable or least wary; the wolf analogy is clear. Although it seems that it was the English-speaking allies who regularly used the term 'wolf pack' (only two of the 135 operational U-boat groups formed during the war had wolf names – *Wolf* and *Werwolf*), the image was clear to Germans and a history of the U-boats in

1955 celebrates this in its original title, *Die Wölfe und der Admiral* (*The Wolves and the Admiral*). The author also clearly plays on the long-established image of attacking wolves:

> That night he intercepted a signal from *U 110*, commanded by Lemp, reporting a convoy from Canada eastward-bound off Iceland. Kretschmer immediately gave chase and Schepke in *U 100* also joined the hunt; both boats attacked by night, sweeping like ravening wolves through a flock of sheep.[31]

At the highest level these wolf packs were under the command of Adolf Hitler who enveloped himself, both personally and militarily, with wolfish terms. It seems that he was proud that his first name could be related to the Old German Athalwolf, which could be rendered as 'Noble Wolf', and he later had his sister change her name to Paula Wolf. In his writings early in his political career he used the pseudonym 'Herr Wolf'. To Winifred Wagner, daughter-in-law of his favourite composer, Richard Wagner, he identified himself on the telephone as 'Conductor Wolf' and her term of endearment for him was 'Wolfie'.

In a newspaper article in 1922 Hitler wrote that the German people had realized 'that a wolf has been born, destined to burst upon the herd of seducers and deceivers of the people'; he, of course, was that wolf of salvation. This is a reversal of the biblical image of the dangerous, ravening wolf attacking a defenceless flock. Here it is the 'herd' that is evil and the wolf the creature from outside that will destroy them. However, he would not do so on his own and later Hitler reportedly referred to the ss as 'My pack of wolves'. In keeping with this imagery, three of Hitler's headquarters from which he planned his predations had wolfish names: in France he had the *Wolfsschult* (Wolf's

76

Bolschewismus
heisst
die Welt im Blut ersäufen.
Vereinigung zur Bekämpfung des Bolschewismus - Berlin W. 9 - Schellingstr. 2.

Gulch), in Ukraine the *Werewolf* and in East Prussia the *Wolfs-schanze* (Wolf's Lair). At the end of his life, hidden away in his Berlin bunker, he still associated himself with the wolf theme, naming one of the pups of Blondi, his favourite German Shepherd dog, Wolf, a creature that only he was permitted to touch.[32]

The wolf continues to serve as an emblem and identity for military and paramilitary units. Some associate themselves with the creature because of wolves' perceived behaviour, particularly their endurance, tenacity, strength and cooperation when hunting. The Spetsnaz, for example, the secretive Russian special forces equivalent to the British sas, have been likened to wolves:

> unofficially the *spetsnaz* badge is a wolf . . . The wolf lives in a pack, a closely knit and well organised fighting unit of frightful predators. The tactics of the wolf pack are the very embodiment of flexibility and daring. The wolves' tactics are an enormous collection of various tricks and combinations, a mixture of cunning and strength, confusing manoeuvres and sudden attacks. No other animal in the world could better serve as a symbol of the *spetsnaz*.[33]

Other modern combat forces both use and generate cultural images that have been explored above. Images of wilderness and wildness, outsiders and outlawry, unregulated cruelty and ferocious violence and a glorification of killing that comes, as it were, naturally, have been part of the identities of usually right-wing, nationalist political groups. The Grey Wolves of Turkey (an unofficial organization of the ultra right-wing Nationalist Movement Party) has been responsible for assassinations and other acts of violent terror. During the early 1990s the Balkan Wars created the conditions for the birth of various packs of human wolves. Perhaps the most notorious were the Serb

paramilitary White Wolves and Wolves of Vucjak, which terrorized and tortured non-Serbs in Croatia and Bosnia.

Militant white supremacist groups, such as the Connecticut White Wolves in the USA and the British White Wolves, also appropriated the image of the wolf to create fear and attack those they believed could be hunted down as though they were mere prey. In 1999 the British White Wolves, which took its name from the Serbian pack, used stereotypical images of wolves in written death threats: 'When the clocks strike midnight on the 31st of December 1999 the White Wolves will begin to howl and when the Wolves begin to howl the Wolves begin to hunt. You have been warned. Hail Britannia.'[34]

In all of these cases centuries-old imaginings of the wolf and the wolf pack have been used to create a fearsome image of human groups in pursuit of their enemies – a case of Plautus' comment '*Lupus est homo homini, non homo*' (One man to another is a wolf, not a man). Although the wolf here is a purely human creation, this particular image and linkage of wolves and humans has been a significant problem for wolves. What humans do to other humans when they act in supposedly wolf-like ways is no more than being human. Unfortunately for wolves, humans have needed and used the wolf to express emotions and behaviours that they could not, or did not wish to, accept or depict as uniquely human. Unfortunately for wolves, their cultural image has also resulted in a uniquely human campaign against wolves themselves.

3 Lupicide

The millennia-old fear of the wolf went hand-in-hand with hatred. Their predation on valuable domestic livestock, hunting of wild animals that the elite wished to preserve for their own sport, and the fear of possible wolf predations on humans created an image of the wolf as an enemy of humankind that should be killed wherever it intruded into human concerns. The result of this construction of wolves is that, until comparatively recently, the wolf has had few human supporters and its fate has largely been persecution and eradication.

Charlemagne was probably the first monarch to order the systematic control of wolves when, in 812, he founded the Louveterie, an elite institution charged with the killing of wolves in royal forests. A century later, in an attempt to control wolf numbers in Anglo-Saxon Britain, dead wolves were converted into a form of tribute. King Edgar (*reg* 959–75), for example, demanded that his Welsh subjects produce 300 wolfskins a year and in England he commuted the punishment of some criminals to a payment of wolf tongues. Other laws, such as Canute's Forest Laws (1016), permitted anyone to kill the creatures outside royal forests. It was not legal to kill them within such forests, but if anyone did, the law said that they would be treated gently. Later, members of the English aristocracy and ecclesiastical authorities paid specialist wolf hunters to kill any they could find. After

Johann Georg Hertel, *Loup pris au piege* (Wolf caught in a leg-hold trap), 18th century, etching.

'Wolf Shooting', the coat of arms for Wolfenschiessen, Switzerland.

relentless persecution, wolves were probably eradicated from England during the reign of Henry VII (1485–1509). In Scotland, especially during the reign of James I, when a law was passed in 1427 enforcing wolf hunts, the aristocracy were commanded to organize communal wolf hunts several times a year and bounties were paid to any other individuals who killed them. Although there is some debate about when the last wolf was killed in Scotland, they had probably been wiped out by the 1680s. Wolves lasted longer in Ireland, where they were regarded as such a menace that in 1652 Oliver Cromwell, in a *Declaration against transporting of Wolffe Dogges*, prohibited the export of wolfhounds. This was supplemented in 1653 with a series of different bounty payments for male and female wolves as well as for wolf pups. Although the last bounty was paid in 1710, wolves seem to have held on in Ireland until nearly the end of the eighteenth century, when there are many accounts of the last wolf in different regions of the country.

Similar stories of systematic attempts to rid the land of a dangerous predator can be found across Europe. Wolves were caught in traps, snares and pits; bounties were paid to encourage local people to hunt them down and professional wolf hunters were paid wages to do the same. By the nineteenth century wolves had been eradicated or reduced to meagre numbers in restricted areas in Scandinavia, Denmark, Switzerland, France, much of Germany, Italy and Spain. In Eastern Europe wolves were hunted hard to reduce their numbers, but this region could

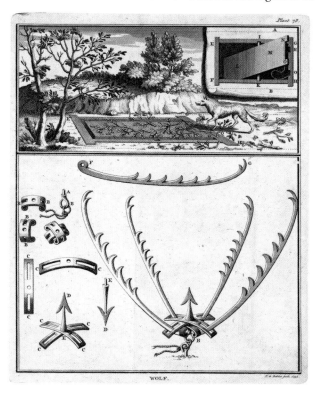

F. De Bakker, 'Wolf', 1742, engraving depicting a complex pit trap for wolves.

always be repopulated from further east, where the vastness of wilderness territory meant that people were never able to erad-icate wolves.[1]

Although there have long been aggressive campaigns against wolves almost wherever they appear, most have taken the form of ambushes, skirmishes and the occasional battle. It required a new hatred on a new continent, combined with new technol-ogical abilities, for this old enmity of humans for wolves to be turned into an all-out war, an attempt at the systematic and total eradication of the species.

When *Homo sapiens* and *Canis lupus* were first living in the same landscapes of North America, any relationship between them was unlikely to be similar to that in the Old World once the processes of domestication of animals for human use were under-way. Indigenous peoples in North America did not domesticate

animals, other than the dogs used for hunting and guarding and, in some cultures and terrains, for pulling sled-like vehicles. These peoples certainly domesticated plants and practised horticulture and agriculture, but in such systems it would be wild herbivores, and perhaps bears, that might be intruding and destructive animals, not wolves. So for thousands of years, societies of wolves and societies of humans hunted the abundant wildlife together. This is not to suggest that the indigenous peoples did not hunt wolves, but such hunting was mostly utilitarian for the purposes to which the dead wolf, its pelt for garments and other parts for medicinal or ritual purposes could be put. Hunting was not undertaken in order to remove an unwanted intruder. The difference from the context of husbandry is important.

The conditions for a revolutionary change in relationships between humans and wild animals in North America came about because Europeans, with very different cultural and agricultural systems, established themselves there. The early settlers set about creating forms of agriculture that brought them into direct conflict with wolves. Most significantly they brought with them domesticated livestock and introduced them into environments that had previously had no such creatures in them and the settlers little understood. What they introduced were new potential prey for wild predators. From the establishment of the first colonies, settlers, supported by local and later state and federal laws and funds, began what was to become a concerted campaign of wolf destruction, driven by frustration, anger and unremitting loathing for wolves. At its height it was pursued with a ruthless and relentless efficiency. Early settlers thought it would be impossible to rid themselves of wolves – 'There is little hope of their utter destruction . . . they may be the greatest inconvenience the Countrey hath'[2] – yet wolves were practically exterminated in the 'Countrey' of New England by the end of the eighteenth century. By the time of the enactment of the Federal Endangered Species Act of 1973, which gave protected status to

Peter Paul Rubens,
Wolf and Foxhunt,
c. 1615–21, oil
on canvas.

wolves, they had been removed from all of the lower 48 states of the USA, leaving just small populations in north-eastern Minnesota and on Isle Royale.

During the Colonial period some 540,000 people migrated from Europe to North America. The largest number came from England (with significant numbers also from Scotland, Ulster, Ireland and Wales); others came from Germany, the Netherlands, France and Sweden. Wolves were possibly still present in the latter countries when the immigrants left, but certainly those from England would have been unlikely to have ever encountered a wolf because they had already been exterminated. Even though the last wolves in Scotland and Ireland were not killed until later, at the time of mass immigration there were likely to have been only small remnant populations of wolves and immigrants from these countries probably had little or no experience of them. Settlers in North America soon became aware of the presence of real wolves close to their farms and settlements. Although they might not have experienced wolves, they certainly had views and ready emotional responses derived from the stories and beliefs outlined in chapter Two: wolves were dangerous, ravenous and evil creatures and they needed to be destroyed to protect people from their predation.

Wolves were demonized immediately. They became a potent symbol of the dangerous, fearful and godless wilderness that surrounded the settlers and threatened the physical safety of their fragile homes and the order of their social and religious communities. Real wolves preyed on livestock and might attack humans, but they also became associated with wider fears of cultural attack from both outside and within. Communities were likened to biblical flocks of sheep that needed protection from wolf attacks and religious and community leaders likened themselves to shepherds who offered such protection. John

Anon., Russian travellers defending themselves again a wolf pack attack, *c.* late 19th century.

Winthrop of Massachusetts, for example, described himself in a letter as 'a poor shepherd . . . among the small flock of sheep I daily fold in this distant part of the wilderness . . . to secure them from the wild rapacious quadrupeds of the forest'.[3] From the outside these creatures of the Devil were associated with the godless savage humans who shared the wilderness with them and suffered similar campaigns of eradication. One pastor described New England in 1662 as 'A waste and *howling* wilderness / Where none inhabited / But hellish fiends, and brutish men / That Devils Worshipped'.[4] But wolves were not just outside, threatening from the edges of civilization. They were also inside and preachers railed against the godless, the irreligious and false believers in their communities as being like wolves in their midst. Cotton Mather, for example, a prominent Boston preacher and one of the most influential religious leaders of his time, wrote a pamphlet in 1691 titled *Little Flocks Guarded Against Grievous Wolves*.

The wolves of the wilderness surrounding the settlements provided a powerful metaphor for religious concerns but it was the threat they were seen to pose to the livelihoods of the communities that led to their persecution. The few livestock that the early settlers brought with them were immensely valuable, but they were also vulnerable to attack by wild carnivores because their owners were often unable to look after them properly in these new environments. Coming from places without wolves, they had no experience of how to protect themselves. Adults were busy learning how to cultivate the plants that were essential for their survival and could not spare the time to tend their animals. Pigs, cows and sheep were therefore either left to their own devices or were looked after by inexperienced children.[5] In such circumstances, away from the settlements, they were easily preyed upon. But such attacks did not mean that wolves were simply classified as pests, a nuisance or even vermin that had to be controlled – instead they were brought into a much more complex social and cultural system of crime, vengeance and punishment. Domesticated animals were the property of their human owners and their loss to wolves was not perceived as an inevitable fact of living in a new and difficult environment, but rather as deliberate theft. Although the loss could not be recovered, nor perhaps could the particular culprit be apprehended as in the case of a human thief, measures could be taken against all potential perpetrators of such crimes. The settlers turned to the old European institution of the bounty, a payment made for the killing of dangerous wild animals or apprehending or killing criminals. Wolves were not simply hunted: they were hunted down. Their criminal identity was confirmed by putting dead wolves on public display, as was sometimes done with executed criminals in Europe.

The first bounty on wolves in North America was established by the Court of Assistants in Boston on 9 November 1630: 'Every

English man that killeth a wolf in any part within the limits of this patent shall have allowed him 1d [1 penny] for every beast & horse, & ob [halfpenny] for every weaned swine & goat in every plantation, to be levied by the constables of the said plantations.'[6] All members of the community who owned livestock made a payment to the hunter for his services. Although this bounty was repealed in 1632, it was re-enacted in 1635 with the bounty raised to five shillings, and by 1637 it had risen to ten shillings. The bounty was now a payment made by the authorities rather than levied on individuals. Once again the bounty was repealed in 1638, and reintroduced in 1640 when 40 shillings was offered for each wolf killed by hounds and ten shillings for each killed using a gun, trap or other instrument. Further repeals and re-enactments followed regularly, perhaps related to whether wolves were felt to be increasing or decreasing their depredations. In all, twelve separate pieces of bounty legislation were enacted in the territory of the Massachusetts Bay Company between 1630 and 1648. It is significant how aspects of this legislation were framed in terms of how the threat from wolves and the nature of their destructive activities were perceived. Bounties were only to be paid out for wolves actually killed within specific territorial jurisdictions. The authorities were concerned not with wolves in general but with the intrusion of wolves into their particular territories and communities. How the authorities ensured that the money paid out was for a wolf killed within their territory was to prove a difficult administrative problem because hunters would sometimes kill a wolf in one place but take it to the authorities of another where a higher bounty was being paid. They would also offer part of a wolf to claim their reward but sell another part of the same wolf elsewhere. Parts of domestic dogs and coyotes were also presented as wolves to easily fooled officials. Some hunters, it was

Dr.   Appropriation for Killing Wolves

			Amount bro't forward		1904	00
1838						
May 21	283	To Warrants	to Wm. Boell, Dan Rhoads & J. M. Mearn		8	00
"	"	To	to J. P. Gillis, P. Calvin & J. Lawrence		3	50
"	"	To	to John Smith		1	00
"	"	To	to Anderson Helm			50
"	"	To	to George Smith			50
"	"	To	to Stephen Anderson		1	00
28	"	To	to William Haley			50
June 1	284	To	to William Lewis		15	00
2	"	To	to Sigler H. Suter		2	00
"	"	To	to Alfred Evans		1	00
4	"	To	to Hooper Morain		5	00
5	"	To	to Isaac Crabtree, Jos Bridges & James Sawyer		8	50
"	"	To	to Robt. J. Williamson, Abraham Winson & Geo. A. Vaughon		4	50
"	285	To	to Reese Williams, Alfred Norris & James Johnson		6	00
"	"	To	to William P. Pitchford & Hiram Lawrence		1	50
"	"	To	to James Denny		1	00
"	"	To	to Henry Hoalt		3	50
5	"	To	to Joseph Campbell & Thomas Hews		3	00
"	"	To	to John Gaston & John Haws		3	00
"	287	To	to Calvin Card & Wm Pruitt		5	50
6	"	To	to Jacob Hinkle		4	00
"	"	To	to John Bice		4	00
"	"	To	to Hiram Robbins & Wm Ray		5	00
"	"	To	to James Simpson & J. M. Beckindall		3	00
"	"	To	to Thomas H. Daughter		5	50
"	288	To	to Geo. M. Hanson & Wm Collum		5	60
13	289	To	to Isaac Enloe & John W. Smith		3	00
"	"	To	to John Causvey			50
"	"	To	to James H. Brown		1	00
"	"	To	to William Snow			50
23	290	To	to John Yarbrough		1	00
30	"	To	to Nicholas H. H. H.			50
July 2	292	To	to John Ellis		4	50
4	293	Do	to M. Richards and others		3	00
7	294	Do	to William C. Ward			50
13	295	Do	to John Alston and others		7	50
14	296	Do	to Thomas Armstrong		3	00
"	"	Do	to James A. Brown			50
20	297	Do	to Tillie Crtchon and Silas Blair		1	00
21	"	Do	to George John and Isaac John		5	50
"	"	Do	to Albert Allen and others		3	00
24	298	Do	to Hardy Foster		3	50
27	"	Do	to Henry Moore & James A. Middleton		6	00
28	"	Do	to John Morris		1	00

The State of Ohio } ss.
Champaign County }
personally came before me Samuel McIlvain
one of the Justices of the peace for S.ᵈ County George
Moore Sen.ʳ of Pike Township and complied with
all the Requesits of the law in proving that
he killed two full grown wolves for which he
is entitled to Receive $8 Certifyed by me this
29 day of Sept.ᵇᵉʳ 1812 — Sam.ˡ McIlvain

Letter authorizing a bounty payment of $8 to a hunter for killing two adult wolves, Ohio, 1812.

claimed, did not kill many females or young because they wanted to ensure a regular supply of wolves to be killed and hence a regular income.

Despite the potential for abuse, wolf bounty legislation was enacted for the next 300 years or so across most of the American states and Canadian provinces. Millions of dollars were spent in the attempt to eradicate wolves. Government-funded bounties were still being paid as late as 2007 in Alaska, where hunters were paid $150 for each wolf killed. The wolf is the only animal with a criminal reputation and record that has lasted for centuries and resulted in so many legal acts putting a price on its head.[7]

The measures taken against the wolf in the period of early settlement could be characterized as defensive, an anxiety about local protection rather than a campaign of systematic extermination taken into, and fought in, the habitat of wolves. The authorities that levied the bounties on wolves would only pay for killing those within their territory and there was no attempt to encourage hunters to pursue and kill wolves in the wilderness.

The settlers wanted to keep wolves away from their livestock and kill those that were close enough to threaten them. Although the protection of domestic animals was a primary concern, wolf behaviour and human interests soon clashed over wild animals.

Most of the early colonists went to North America to escape forms of social structures, controls and restrictions; they arrived seeking new freedoms and with expectations of developing new ways of living. The land to which they came was, as it were, a blank canvas on which they could create, in their imagination, a desired world. But it was also a physical reality they had to contend with in order to realize this desire. In the main their method of doing this was to impose themselves on it, to take control, rather than to insert themselves into it and work with it. Although the wilderness was configured in the colonists' imagination as a feared and fearful expanse in which all sorts of dangers lurked and as a place that had to be subdued and dominated if they were ever to bring civilization to their new homeland, there were some benefits to be gained from it.

The forests were obviously a source of essential timber for fuel and building but they also harboured valuable wildlife. When the numbers of imported domestic livestock were only gradually being built up, the colonists needed other sources of meat and they turned to the abundant and, importantly, freely available herds of deer and other wild herbivores. Most of the colonists would not have been permitted to hunt deer in their native countries, for these were classified as 'game' and protected by strict laws that allowed them to be killed only by members of rural elites in highly ritualized hunts. In the woods that surrounded the colonists' settlements deer had no such status and no elite protectors or owners. They were public property and could be, and were, hunted by anyone with the means to kill them. This abundant wildlife could have withstood harvesting as part of a subsistence economy as it had done for as long as the creatures had been hunted by indigenous peoples. The problem was that the colonists quickly began to exploit them, mainly for their furs and hides, with deer and other wild animals entering a commercial, and ultimately unsustainable, economy. From the end of the seventeenth century colonies had to impose deer hunting regulations, particularly closed season regulations, in an attempt to allow numbers to recover. Hunters disliked such restrictions and were intensely resentful of other predators. In this context the colonists did not regard the wolves that preyed on deer as doing something entirely natural; rather they were hated as rivals taking resources that belonged to them. Even though the wild deer were not the private property of particular individuals, they were certainly perceived as the exclusive property of humans: there for the benefit of people, not savage animal predators. In 1633 William Hammond wrote, 'Here is good store of deer; were it not for the wolves here would be abound, for the does have most two fawns at once, and some have three, but the wolves destroy them.'[8] As will be explored later, wolves were not only persistently blamed for killing livestock: they were also blamed, as if they were acting in an inappropriate manner, for killing buffalo, deer, elk, moose and anything else that humans wanted to kill for food or sport. The settlers simply could not tolerate rival predators.

It was when people crossed, and began to settle in, the western plains in the nineteenth century that wolf hatred and killing in North America entered a new phase. This killing was of a different order from that of colonial times, when there were few professional wolf hunters who only lived from bounties and the killing was both haphazard and artisanal. In the nineteenth century large numbers became professional wolf hunters and they were able to be systematic and intensive in their killing

ROYAL CANADIAN MOUNTED POLICE

(C.I.B.)

In Reply Please Quote

Div.File No. 32 W.650-1028

H.Q. File No..............

Winnipeg, Man. August 18th, 1932.

R.McN. Pearson, Esq.
Deputy Provincial Treasurer,
Parliament Bldgs.,
Winnipeg, Man.

Sir:-

Re: Fred PIPEEN - St. Lazare, Man.
Obtaining money by False Pretences.
Sec. 405 C.C.C.

For your information, I enclose herewith, copy of Russell Detachment report of the 11th inst. re the above, from which you will note that this man has been arrested and charged with obtaining money by false pretences—for having obtained from the Rural Municipality of Ellice the sum of $14.00 for Wolf bounty on rabbit skins which he had made to appear as genuine wolf pelts. You will also note that he has made a complete confession of his actions, and also implicated several others, one of whom has also been arrested, and efforts are being made to locate and apprehend the others.

It would appear to me that there should be some change in the manner of paying Wolf bounties, and it should be made necessary that the whole of the pelt be produced before any bounty would be paid, and also that the Municipalities should be advised that greater care should be taken by the persons receiving applications for Wolf bounty, for it seems to me that if a reasonable examination were made of the pelts, a rabbit pelt could easily be detected from that of a Wolf pelt. If the person taking applications for Wolf bounty and passing same, and taking the necessary affidavit, was made responsible for any loss for bounty which had been obtained illegally, that person would exercise greater care, and would make sure that the pelts in question were Wolf pelts.

There is trouble every year in connection with the payment of Wolf Bounty, on account of persons offering Wolf pelts, either by sewing on ears after the original have been cut off, and so obtaining bounty on the same pelts on more than one occasion, and much of this could be prevented by a little more careful examination of the pelts at the time the bounty is applied for, and I think it would be advisable that the Municipalities be warned to take greater care in this connection.

I will advise you of the result of the prosecutions in the present instances.

through the use of industrial products deliberately produced for this purpose – poison (particularly strychnine) and specially designed metal wolf traps.

Once again the attitudes to wolves and relationships with them developed in the context of human relations with other animals, this time the buffalo. The first people to explore the plains commented on the immensity and density of buffalo herds and on the vast numbers of wolves that could be seen around the herds. Some were apprehensive about the wolves that often came close to their camps, seemingly unperturbed by human presence, and were unnerved by wolves howling at night, but there is little sense in the written record that wolves needed to be controlled. There is, however, evidence of a continuation of the view that wild predators should not intrude into human interests. It

John Burley Waring, 'Hunting Group in Bronze', 1823–75, chromo-lithograph reproduction of a sculpture of the same title by Nicholas Liberich.

seems that once humans had declared an interest in a particular wild animal then they and they alone should be the rightful agents of its death. Wolves were certainly blamed for the decline of the buffalo. For example, a nineteenth-century naturalist complained:

Formerly [wolves] everywhere harassed the buffalo, destroying many of the young, and even worrying and finally killing, and devouring the aged, feeble and the wounded. Thirty years since wolves, next to the Indians, were the greatest scourge of the buffaloes, and had no small degree in effecting their decrease.[9]

Although they were blamed for the decimation of the herds of buffalo, not even the largest and most efficient packs could have killed so extensively and intensively. This 30 years coincided with the beginning of the newly arrived European frontier people's realization that the buffalo could be valuable. Indigenous peoples had exploited the buffalo herds for hundreds of years, as had wolves, but this did not significantly reduce their numbers. What signified the end for the buffalo was that it swiftly shifted from being an animal that formed part of a subsistence economy to one that, like the deer in the east, entered a national and international commercial economy.

Buffalo were certainly shot for meat by frontier people but they were not particularly valued except for their tongues and their skins. Buffalo tongue became a delicacy in the growing cities of the east and buffalo hides were used for blankets, clothing and boots. With a buoyant market for these buffalo parts, hundreds of men moved to the plains to become buffalo hunters, although with powerful rifles and the density of the herds this was scarcely hunting and much more akin to an open-air slaughterhouse, with some hunters regularly killing several hundred a day. Buffalo were shot, their valuable parts removed and the carcasses left to rot and become an easy source of food for wolves and other scavengers.

Nineteenth- and early twentieth-century writers estimated the numbers of buffalo on the plains in the 1830s as being anywhere between ten million and 100 million, although more modern scientific calculations suggest a figure somewhere between 27 and 30 million, still an impressive number. By the early 1880s, though, the species was near extinction.[10] Environmental factors might have played their part in this decline but, in the main, the buffalo was brought to the point of extinction by the rifle.

What is significant about this period for wolves is that the last twenty years of the decimation of the buffalo herds was a time in which the wolf was sought out because it had become a valuable commodity. From the 1860s to the 1880s wolves were killed in large numbers not simply because they attacked domestic livestock or the buffalo but because there was a market for their fur. Wolves had been trapped in North America for the fur trade during the late eighteenth century, but after that period wolf furs were out of fashion in Europe and commercial wolf trapping on a large scale was hardly viable. However, by the mid-nineteenth century the price for wolfskins began to increase – in large part due to demand from the Russian army for wolf fur for coats – and it became worthwhile for hunters to spend time catching them. This was a period in which wolves became valuable and a means for killing them in great numbers became available. It was the intensity of the slaughter of buffalo and the littering of the plains with their carcasses that, in part, enabled the wolfers, as they came to be known, to kill their prey in such great numbers. Just as the buffalo hunters did not really have to hunt buffalo, neither did the wolfers need much skill to kill wolves. They did not have to track them or be good marksmen

98

AMERICAN BUFFALO

PLATE XLV. UNGULATA.

because wolf killing in this period did not require any close engagement with wolves; they were simply poisoned and the poison was, in the main, placed in the buffalo carcasses that were scavenged.

Strychnine, obtained from the seeds of the *Nux vomica* tree for the control of vermin, was exported from Europe to North America and used, although not extensively, in the Colonial period. It was in the nineteenth century that strychnine became a formidable weapon in the war against wolves. In 1834 Rosengarten & Sons, a pharmaceutical company in Philadelphia, began the manufacture of strychnine on an industrial scale and the wholesale availability of the poison allowed wolfers to kill easily and in great numbers. Once again there was an unfortunate coincidence for wolves. Strychnine was most effective in cold conditions and wolfers needed to kill wolves in the winter when their fur was most luxuriant. The poison was put into buffalo carcasses left by buffalo hunters, into buffalo shot by wolfers or into other forms of bait such as beef suet. All the wolfers had to do was to visit the site of poisoning the next morning and look for the dead wolves. Because fatal strychnine poisoning commences within a few minutes of ingestion, with the muscles beginning to contract, then going into spasm, and finally the whole body shaken by convulsions, the poisoned wolf would not be able to travel far. Wolfers reported being able to kill many dozens in this way in one night and this became a highly profitable enterprise. A monument, of a grisly kind, to this mass killing of wolves was built during 1871 near Sun City in Kansas. A French pioneer settler, L. C. Fouquet, in a letter written 50 years later describing buffalo hunting, reported that close to a wolfers' village 'was a road going thro the swampy creek valley, about 75 yards wide, and this had been artistically and scientifically paved with gray wolve carcasses and I drove over this bone road several times'.[11]

Wolf killing in the latter part of the nineteenth century was not motivated by concerns about protection or eradication, but by the profit that could be made from the wolves themselves. About the same time as the demise of the buffalo herds, there was a decline in the market for wolf pelts, but this did not mean that wolf killing ceased. Rather it increased and this time the motivation certainly was destruction and eradication. Cattle were introduced in huge numbers into the spaces previously occupied by buffalo, and wolves unsurprisingly, because they had lost their traditional prey, began to attack these new herds. This predation was intolerable to ranchers and they instigated an all-out war. It was not simply that ranchers resented the economic loss they suffered from wolves killing their livestock: their feelings were far more powerful and personal than that. Ranchers lost animals to disease, while droughts and extreme winters could decimate flocks and herds; these were accepted as part of the harsh realities of the natural world and ranching life. What were not accepted as natural were attacks by wolves on animals on the open range or, even worse, in corrals.

Not surprisingly livestock owners were angry at their financial losses: many claimed that they lost more than 10 per cent of their herd and sometimes up to 50 per cent of calves a year to wolves. But they were also outraged by the ways in which wolves killed their animals. Many claimed that wolves took pleasure in killing animals that they often did not bother to eat; others complained about what they called 'bob-tailing', a process by which a wolf would seize a fleeing steer by the tail and, using the swing of the tail, wrench it off. However, what particularly angered ranchers was the classic form of wolf attack in which several wolves would surround an animal, snapping and ripping at it until it finally collapsed. This was seen to reveal the wolf at its most vicious, devouring a defenceless creature while

it was still alive. Clearly, ranchers wanted to protect their herds from such attacks but their response was not a simple defensive campaign to keep wolves away. Ranchers responded as though it was a deliberate personal attack and the harm they suffered could only be responded to by demands of vengeance. As the historian Edward Curnow puts it, the wolf became 'an object of pathological hatred' and in their individual and collective fury the ranchers launched a formidable attack against the entire species.[12]

The demand by ranchers for eradication of all wolves was also, in a sense, exported from the United States, as were the skills and expertise necessary for mass wolf killing. In the latter part of the nineteenth century Japanese government officials were keen to develop scientific animal husbandry in the form of ranching cattle and horses on Hokkaido. They turned to the USA as the model for such an enterprise and in 1873 Edwin Dun, a rancher from Ohio, arrived in Japan to advise on the project. For centuries wolves had been revered and worshipped in Japan, particularly by indigenous hunters and farmers. However, when wolves began to intrude by preying on large numbers of horses and cattle, their divinity slipped from them and, as in America, they became pests whose presence could not be tolerated. Wolves had been hunted to control their numbers but the arrival of ranching brought with it Western attitudes to wolves and the demand for lupicide. According to Brett Walker,

> Whereas in the seventeenth and eighteenth centuries peasants revered wolves at Shinto shrines as guardians of Tokagawa agriculture or reviled them as 'mad' demons, the Meiji regime ruled out both of these 'primitive' interpretations in favor of modern Western ones and categorized wolves as 'noxious animals.[13]

Dunn brought to Japan his knowledge of the power of bounties and the efficacy of traps and strychnine. To ensure the success of this project of modernity, what Walker neatly terms 'ecologies of progress', a term that could equally be applied to nineteenth-century America, the wolves of Hokkaido were systematically exterminated.

A similar attempt at local wolf control, although total eradication was the ideal, was also taking place in Russia. Here the wolf had been demonized for centuries for its predations on domesticated and game animals. Wolves had been hunted down by peasants and collective wolf drives had attempted to clear areas. What had also continued into the nineteenth century were organized wolf hunts by mounted gentry and aristocrats who pursued and killed wolves with packs of borzoi hounds. This was a protective service to their peasants but also a highly regarded form of sport. By the mid-nineteenth century, though, with the decline of the rural aristocracy and the abolition of serfdom, this form of hunting to control wolf numbers had declined and was ineffective.

At the same time the Russian government was concerned with understanding the economic impact of wolf predations and to solve the wolf problem in the most effective way. V. M. Lazareveski was commissioned to investigate the extent of wolf predation and put a cost to it. He concluded, after reviewing the official records, that across Russia almost 750,000 domestic animals had been killed by wolves in 1873 alone. His suggestion, published as *On the Destruction of Domesticated Livestock and Wild Game by Wolves and on the Eradication of Wolves* (1876), was that hunting was ineffective and that Russia should begin the systematic use of strychnine. His pamphlet provoked debate among hunters, some of whom suggested that an eradication of wolves would signal the end of the traditional skills of hunting. Others argued for mixed methods of control – hunting, bounties, mandatory communal hunts and poisoning. On 3 February 1892 the government promulgated a major new hunting act that 'codified this collective cultural animus against wolves and other predators'. Permission was given to kill all predatory animals and birds at any time of the year and 'Provincial and district authorities are authorized to permit the use of poison as a universal measure for the extermination of predatory animals or to permit individuals or hunting societies to employ it.'[14]

In the USA bounties re-emerged as a way of encouraging participation in this war against wolves and later the powerful livestock associations were able to force government agencies to invest in the killing. Strychnine was still regularly used in huge quantities against wolves and it was almost a law of the range that every cowboy should carry a pouch of strychnine and should not pass an animal carcass without stopping to lace it with poison. This extensive use of poison finally began to yield diminishing returns and it was reported that wolves were becoming ever more

Cover of a booklet advertising the Newhouse trap, c. 1857.

NEWHOUSE TRAP

STANDARD
OF THE WORLD
FOR 60 YEARS

FOR PROFESSIONAL TRAPPERS nothing can replace the time-tested Newhouse Traps. Every trap is guaranteed perfect. Sure to go, sure to hold.

ONEIDA COMMUNITY LTD., - ONEIDA, N.Y.

wary of baited meat. However, such was the demand for effective wolf killing that a new weapon was soon available. Metal traps designed specifically for wolves had long been available in North America, although they had been of local, craft production, often made by blacksmiths. Now that ranchers needed traps in large numbers there was a company ready to supply them.

The most famous trap-maker was Sewell Newhouse, who began to develop a range of animal traps in 1823 and continued his home-made production into the 1840s. His traps were in great demand because his mastery of tempering springs ensured that the traps held their prey. In 1849 he joined the recently established Oneida religious community in Madison County, New York. Initially this was a community based on agricultural production but in 1856, because of demand for traps, Newhouse and J. H. Noyes began small-scale factory production of a range of sophisticated specialist traps. Newhouse's early traps had sold at a rate of some 2,000 a year but sales now rose to nearly 10,000 a year. This industrial production of traps was celebrated by the manufacturers as a means of extracting a profit from the wilderness by capturing valuable fur-bearing animals and as an essential tool for conquering and civilizing the wilderness by controlling wild predators.

The Newhouse 4½ Wolf Trap was developed in response to the demand from ranchers for specialist wolf traps. A company pamphlet described the trap, which was connected to a 1.5-m (5-ft) long drag chain, as being powerful enough to hold a pull of 900 kg (2,000 lb). Included was an article by the eminent naturalist and writer of animal stories Ernest Thompson Seton, describing techniques for disguising and setting the traps and encouraging each hunter to purchase at least 100 of these traps, which sold for $35 a dozen without chains and $40 a dozen with chains. The fame and evocative (although no longer trapping) power of these devices continues and an original Newhouse 4½ Wolf Trap in good condition will easily fetch several hundred dollars at auction.

Although the deaths of wolves were sought, the traps were not designed to kill. These were leg hold traps and wolves that were unable to drag themselves away with the trap attached, or gnaw through their caught legs to escape, had to wait for the trappers to come and kill them. It was this conjunction – a trapped wolf and a man with the means of killing it immediately and swiftly – that reveals something crucial about the relationships between humans and wolves at the time. Trappers reported that caught wolves rarely attempted to attack an approaching human. They were often described as cowering and submissive, a response interpreted as a sign of the innate cowardice of the wolf when alone and confronted by a human. Sometimes the wolf was shot at close range or bludgeoned to death, but frequently the process was much more protracted. Often a captured wolf was released from the trap, tied up alive, its mouth wired or tied shut, thrown over a saddle and taken to a ranch or public space. The bounty hunter brought in the wanted criminal. This was a process that many modern commentators have seen as unnatural, shameful and almost inexplicably cruel, but it also reveals the general loathing for wolves whose behaviour put them too far

'Roping Gray
Wolf', Wyoming,
1887.

'A wolf chase on the Hungarian steppes', Liebig Company advertisement, late 19th century.

beyond the pale of humane treatment. Not only were the hapless creatures displayed to an interested public, with many of the hunters having their pictures taken with them before or after they were shot, but many were beaten, baited with hounds, lassoed and dragged behind galloping horses or pulled apart by two riders on horses; some were even set on fire. This behaviour was a public punishment: vengeance was taken, or justice was seen to be done to animals for which a swift and easy death was thought to be too good.

All wolves were perceived as criminal animals but, as their numbers steadily decreased, a few that continued to kill livestock and outwit their pursuers attained the status and fame of true outlaws. It was claimed that these 'loners' killed more livestock than other wolves and that they did so for the pleasure of demonstrating that they could antagonize humans. Their skills in evading capture, often over many years, became legendary and, significantly, these became named individuals rather than anonymous animals. The lives and deaths of wolves such as

Lobo, the Custer Wolf, Rags the Digger, Old Three Toes, Whitey
of Bear Springs Mesa, Bigfoot, Old Lefty, Split Rock Wolf and
Unaweep were told and embellished as folklore and their histories were written. For example, some claimed that the Custer
Wolf had personally destroyed $25,000 worth of livestock and
that Split Rock Wolf had cost ranchers $10,000, Old Lefty was
held guilty of killing some 384 head of livestock during an eight-
year period and Old Three Toes's toll was more than $50,000 in
losses during a thirteen-year campaign against ranchers, during
which time more than 150 men tried their hand at capturing the
animal. As one writer commented, the Custer Wolf became '90
per cent legend and only 10 per cent animal' and the same pro-
portions of fact and fiction can probably be claimed for the other
creatures.[15] These were extraordinary wolves, hunted down with

a ruthless persistence, but, as with their human counterparts such as Billy the Kid and Jesse James, there was a grudging admiration for these larger-than-life individuals. Those who often spent months hunting individual wolves sometimes expressed themselves in similar terms as responding to a duty to bring a criminal to justice. When asked whether he took any pleasure from capturing a wolf, Bill Caywood, a legendary wolf hunter of the early twentieth century, replied:

> Oh, yes – and no . . . I've just got a lot of love and respect for the gray wolf. He's a real fellow, the big gray is. Lots of brains. I feel sorry for him, It's his way of livin'. He don't know better. And I feel sorry for him every time I see one of those fellows thrashin' in a trap bellowin' bloody murder. Guess I'm too much a part of this outdoors to hold any grudge against animals. It's part the way that wolves go after poor defenceless steers, murder does and fawns and drag down bucks, that helps me go out and bring them in.[16]

An equally famous hunter of the period, Bert Hewa, adds a judicial note to the idea of 'bringing them in'. He expressed regret at having to kill families of wolf pups but then, in response to a rancher who complained about losing so many of his 'calf babies' to such wolves, comments: 'Well that's what makes me stay on the job when a bunch of bad wolves like this are up for extermination. After all, they sign their own death warrant in the blood of cattle.'[17]

The men who brought about the final end of wolves in most states in America were not those who had previously earned money for wolf killing. Some of the previous hunters had been professionals but they had been self-employed, making money

The successful end of a wolf hunt, 1913, photographic postcard.

WOLFHUNT FEB. 3 1913   NO. 106

from wolves where they could but also supporting themselves with other work. The new hunters were salaried government employees and their accounts of how they brought in these legendary, hardened criminals have strong echoes of how other agents, the FBI, justified, romanticized and celebrated their achievements in the human world.[18]

The demand for wolf eradication at the end of the nineteenth century and the beginning of the twentieth was, in large part, driven by local and state livestock owners' associations such as the Wyoming Stock Growers Association (1873), the Texas and Southwestern Cattle Raisers Association (1877) and, later, the National Livestock Association (1898). They offered bounty payments for wolves to which their members contributed. However, they came to feel that as significant contributors of taxes they had the right to help from the government and, as such associations became politically influential, they began to demand federal support for this eradication. Their demand was for a more systematic and effective campaign than the bounty system, which was both patchy in its effectiveness and open to

The wolf targeted as 'varmit' in an advertisement for the Savage 99 rifle in *The American Rifleman*, c. 1950.

Edward A. Goldman and Stanley P. Young, biologists and wolf specialists at the US Bureau of Biological Science. Their two-volume *The Wolves of North America* (1944) is a classic text.

U. S. Biological Survey, and Stanley Young (Left)
Major E. A. Goldman studying skulls to determine the species.
There are a number of geographical races of the wolf differing mainly
in size and cranial characters. Biological Survey collection in U. S. Museum.

fraud and abuse. At the beginning of the twentieth century a peculiar conjunction of processes and practices was established that almost completed the eradication of the wolf in the 48 contiguous states of the USA. These processes, however, also established the conditions and spaces that would later allow the wolf to be re-evaluated and permit the species to re-establish itself in viable populations.

Driven by the livestock owners' associations, the Biological Survey, a governmental organization, employed specialists to conduct major studies, in 1907 and 1909, into predator relations with those animals classed as big game and with livestock. Some of these studies were conducted on private land but the majority were of predator–prey relationships within national parks and forests. The significance of the latter was that livestock owners paid the government grazing fees within these national preserves and they argued that it was the responsibility of the government to protect their stock there.

The first national parks and national forests established in the nineteenth century in the USA were not intended primarily to preserve a newly valued notion of wilderness, although later this did gradually become the guiding ethos of park management. At the beginning it was not wilderness itself but what such wilderness contained that was the central focus of interest. In particular there was a concern to make sure that valuable assets were not exploited by private interests. In terms of wild animal management in national parks, what were perceived as noble or good animals – such as deer, elk and moose – were offered sanctuary and protection against indiscriminate killing. No such protection was offered to predators, which were still seen as essentially destructive forces that intruded into the natural world as humans imagined and wanted it to be. As biologist George Wright wrote about early management philosophies, 'a livestock concept of wildlife administration prevailed', and naturally wolves were still the enemy within such a system.[19] Theodore Roosevelt, hunter, conservationist and sometime president, famously described the wolf as 'the arch type of ravin, the beast of waste and desolation'.[20] Even more scathing was William Hornaday, a key conservationist – or at least protectionist – of certain species, who became director of the New York Zoological Park in 1896: 'Of all the wild creatures of North America none are more despicable than wolves. There is no depth of meanness, treachery, or cruelty to which they do not cheerfully descend.'[21] Later he described the wolf as 'the most degenerate and unmoral mammal species on earth'.[22]

Initially the rangers of the Forest Service (with the help of livestock owners and other hunters) were ordered to kill all

wolves, and in 1907 alone they killed some 1,800 wolves and 23,000 coyotes in and around national parks and forests. In 1914 the Bureau of Biological Survey was authorized to apply for funds from the federal government and in 1915 it was awarded $125,000: the first federal grant given specifically for predator control in national parks and public land. By 1931 approximately three-quarters of the entire budget of the Bureau of Biological Survey was being used for predator control and by then its rangers had poisoned, trapped and shot almost every wolf from all the national parks in the contiguous USA. More widely, between 1900 and 1950 the wolf was made virtually extinct except for viable populations in Alaska and a minimal population of approximately 300 in northern Minnesota.

However, from the 1930s there were some who questioned the slaughter of all wolves and other predators in national parks. Biologists commissioned to study the behaviour of wolves with a view to their more effective control began to develop a greater understanding and appreciation of the social and ecological relations between wolves and the relationships between them and their prey. A set of views began to develop around the idea of a balance of nature in which wolves had a valuable and even essential role to play in maintaining, through their predation, the healthy viability of herds of wild herbivores.

From the mid-twentieth century, driven by both increasingly scientific and popular environmentalism, the general demand for wolf eradication gradually began to give way, albeit at first grudgingly, to a view of the wolf as a native species with an important role to play in the spaces and processes of the wilderness and a rightful place there. Although there were many dissenting voices representing various anti-wolf interest groups, in 1973 the grey wolf was included in The Endangered Species Act in the United States. It was listed as endangered in 47 of the

The appropriate punishment for criminal wolves. Mr W. Yorchuk, Harmony Bay, Ontario, Canada, poses with his trophies, mid-20th century, postcard.

contiguous states and as threatened in Minnesota. Only in Alaska was the wolf population considered to be stable and viable. This measure meant that, with the exception of Alaska, the actions of federal agencies were not allowed to impinge in a detrimental manner on the animals or their habitats and that individuals were not allowed to kill, harm or harass them. Not only did the federal agencies have to avoid harmful or destructive activities, they were also charged with actively conserving wolf populations and working to bring them to a state of viability, when there would no longer be a need to list them as endangered.

Also in 1973 the Wolf Specialist Group of the International Union for the Conservation of Nature and Natural Resources met in Stockholm. The opening of its manifesto could be regarded as the starting point for the re-evaluation of the wolf: 'Wolves, like all other wildlife, have a right to exist in a wild state. This right is in no way related to their known value to mankind. Instead, it derives from the right of all living creatures to co-exist with man as part of the natural ecosystems.' Not only is this a statement of the place of *Canis lupus* as a predator within the ecosystems it inhabits and in which it has a rightful and necessary role, but it also suggests a cultural re-evaluation of the wolf, and all wild animals, as having intrinsic value. This demand, or perhaps plea, for peaceful coexistence would not be achieved solely through rational, scientific, ecological understanding. What was required was the cultural creation of a new wolf in the world: the wolf of lupophilia.

4 Lupophilia

The wolf has not always been feared. Many peoples have treated wolves with respect and associated themselves with what they perceive to be their admirable qualities as powerful, skilled and resilient cooperative hunters. Many of the richest accounts of such respect and admiration come from indigenous North American societies and cultures where respectful and non-antagonistic relations between humans and wolves have existed from the beginning of their histories. Claus Chee Sonny, a modern guardian of a Navajo 'Huntingway', recounts how his people learnt hunting skills from wolves at the beginning of the world. Wolf gave permission to humans to use his voice as the proper way to communicate between themselves when hunting. If they did not speak to each other with his voice they would see deer around them but never manage to shoot one. Sonny tells how Begochidi-woman, Begochidi, Talking-god and Black-god created game animals for hunters and how the hunters had to be instructed in the proper, respectful ways of hunting and killing them. Fawn, in this mythic time, told the hunters that if he was shot and cried out, then bad things would befall the hunters. If, however, they knew the cure then all would be well for them. A song and prayers were created for this situation so that the hunter, having killed, could go in peace.[1]

In the Navajo hunting tradition human hunters took on, or absorbed, attributes of the animal in whose way they hunted; if they hunted in the 'Wolfway' they became wolf-like. Richard Nelson, in his account of how the Koyukon people of Alaska think about and interact with the natural world, also comments on how they recognize the similarities of cooperation involved when humans hunt and when wolves hunt and how the Koyukon express a strong sense of identity with wolves. Once again, such relationships were formed at the beginning of the world, in the Distant Time, when: 'A wolf-person lived among people and hunted with them. When they parted ways, they agreed that wolves would sometimes make kills for people or drive game to them, as a repayment for favors given when wolves were still human.'[2] Since that time Koyukon hunters still claim their rights to wolf kills that they believe have been left for them by the animals but, in a spirit of reciprocity, they also leave parts of their own kills for wolves. That respect exists between Koyukon people and wolves does not mean that wolves are not killed. But, as with all hunting among these people, it was done with respect and high regard for their prey.

Similar elements are reported in the hunting culture of the Ainu people of Japan who, in common with other hunting societies, did not separate their human world from the world of the animals around them; they were all of one world. The Ainu had legends of close relationships between people and wolves, predicated on a deep reverence for wolves. Hunters would leave

Ceremonial wolf mask made by the Tlingit people, Alaska, c. 1867, painted wood.

121

part of their kill and allow wolves to take a share but equally, if a hunter cleared his throat when coming upon wolves feeding, then the wolf god would allow him space at the kill. As with the Koyukon people, the Ainu killed wolves and used their meat and fur but if this were not done in the correct ritual manner or if parts of the wolf were wasted then the pack to which the wolf had belonged would seek out the disrespectful hunter and kill him. It is unclear whether the killing of wolves in this culture was ever a utilitarian act or if it was fundamentally a ritual activity of which meat and fur were by-products. For the Ainu, the wolf was an important deity known as Horkew Kamuy and they would sacrifice wolves in a religious ceremony called 'sending away'. Through this ritual the divine spirit was released from the fleshly wolf so that it could return to the realm of the spirits and from there once more return to animate wolves on earth with divinity.[3]

Many indigenous North American peoples have respected wolves as skilled and admired hunters. In these societies, and in hunting societies generally, wolves were not creatures of terror that intruded in violent and unacceptable ways into human concerns. Consequently there was no need for people to defend themselves against them, let alone to destroy them whenever they were encountered. This notion of intrusion is important here in two senses. In such societies and cultures there was no notion of wilderness as either a physical or cultural environment set apart from humans into which they ventured as into an alien space. As the Lakota writer Joseph Marshal III expressed it: 'There was no operative notion that the area in which they did not live was somehow "wild" or "wilder" than where they did live.'[4] Mountains, forests, plains and tundra were the places they inhabited and the animals they coexisted with there were not 'wild animals', they were simply the animals of those places.

Where they lived, there lived wolves and vice versa. Not only could wolves therefore not intrude spatially, because people were not trying to maintain parts of the landscape for their exclusive use (except perhaps in the limited sense of their camps), neither could they intrude economically, for, without livestock, there was nothing that wolves could take from people. Wolves and humans hunted the same game animals but, with no sense of human ownership of such animals, there was no perception that wolves were competitors who were taking what should be reserved solely for humans.

Some of the richest accounts of the incorporation of admired qualities of wolves into human lives come from the northwestern coastal area of North America, particularly from among the Kwakiutl, Makah, Tlingit and Haida peoples. Here the stamina, bravery and endurance perceived to be exhibited by wolves as hunters of large and potentially dangerous animals such as caribou and moose are transposed into warrior qualities of humans. However, unlike the warrior qualities traced in chapter Two, here there is a sense not of symbolism but of conversation. Various stories from the Nuu-chah-nulth people (previously known as the Nootkan) of Vancouver Island tell how humans approached wolves in order to obtain their power over their enemies. These stories, told in various versions, involve a young man, from among the last members of a tribe that has survived local warfare, gaining access to the home of Wolves in the mountains. In order to do so he has to show great fortitude and endure suffering since he has himself bled in order to remove his human scent. His colleagues then sew him into the skin of a seal and leave him on the beach. The Wolves find him and he is carried to their home. When they cut open the seal, they find the man still alive. The Wolf Chief, admiring the young warrior's bravery, realizes that he would not have endured such hardships unless he desired something very important from them. The man is offered a variety of gifts but what he wants is a war club so powerful that people die simply by looking at it. In fact the man dies several times when in the presence of the club and the Wolves have to bring him back to life before he learns from them how to handle it. He also learns the dances and songs that will later form a crucial part of complex initiation ceremonies. The Wolves accompany him back to his home and he becomes a great leader because of this power. This, however, is a dangerous gift from the Wolves, given only to him because of his personal bravery, and it cannot be passed on to anyone else. When he dies, the club, which he always kept hidden in the woods, is reclaimed by the Wolves.

These origin stories of how the power of wolves came into this society through the achievements of one man were closely linked with initiation ceremonies, known as the Wolf Ritual or

Wolf mask made by the Tlingit people, Alaska, 19th century, wood, human hair, shells and leather.

Klukwalle, in which the secrets of their power were learnt in a ritual process related to key elements of the first warrior's difficult journey. At the heart of these ceremonies was the initiation of novices into secret knowledge through a set of processes involving an oscillation between the world of wolves and the world of humans. The novices were captured by wolves (men who had been initiated) and taken to a house in the woods where they were kept in isolation and given secret knowledge by their wolf captors. During their days of isolation the wolf captors would be heard howling and occasionally would be seen skirting along the edge of the woods. The villagers would attempt to trap these wolves but without success. After several days both wolves and novices would appear on the banks of a river, the villagers would approach and a battle would ensue during which the novices would be wrenched from their captors and returned to the village. Other ceremonies would then be performed to drive away the wolf spirits and to reincorporate the new initiates into human society.

As with the story of obtaining the war club, this ceremony turned on humans being taken by wolves into their world where they are given the secrets of power before being returned to their own world. According to an early analyst of wolf ceremonies in northwestern North America:

> It was stated by informants that the wolf was chosen as the tutelary animal because it was the bravest and fiercest of animals. Certainly, bravery and endurance were among the qualities suggested – or stressed – by various aspects of the ceremonial to its initiated. It is possible that the strengthening of these qualities were among the primal objects of the ceremonial.[5]

Although fierceness is mentioned here, there is no sense in any of the ethnographic accounts of attitudes to wolves among these peoples that they perceived them as ferocious, in the sense of being savage, bloodthirsty and destructive.

A key element in these complex rituals is that the wolves are part of the transformative process of creating people who are able to participate fully in the ritual and ceremonial life of their society. The initiates are taken from the places of human habitation and held in a state of liminality, in a zone of wolf habitation, where the wolves act as their teachers, before they are brought back and reincorporated into the human social world. In one sense this temporary and highly ritualized coexistence of humans and wolves contains an element of animals nurturing young people, something found in other stories of humans raised by wolves.

The most celebrated story, particularly in terms of visual representations, of a wolf nurturing humans is that of the She-wolf and Romulus and Remus. Once again, the legend centres on the transition of people from the spaces of human habitation to the natural domain of wolves, through a period of liminality, before returning to civilization. Indeed, this story is a key element in the origin myth of an entire civilization. However, as Livy comments in his account, this She-wolf could have been a wolf of a very human kind.

His version of the story begins with Amulius, who seized control of the Silvian clan from his brother Numitor, the rightful

Kaviagamute dancers in wolf costume, Alaska, c. 1914.

127

ruler. To maintain his usurpation he had the male sons of his brother killed and made his niece Rhea Silva a vestal virgin, an honour that should have ensured there were no offspring to challenge his rule. However, Rhea was raped and gave birth to twin boys. She claimed that the father was Mars but their divine fathering was no protection. Amulius ordered that they be thrown into the Tiber, but those sent to drown them could not reach the main channel of the river and so left them in a basket in one of the overflows. Instead of being submerged by the flood waters, the waters retreated, leaving the boys on dry land. It was then that

Antoinette Bouzonnet Stella, *Shepherds, watched by a river god and nymphs 'rescue' Romulus and Remus from the She-wolf,* 1675, engraving.

A thirsty she-wolf from the surrounding hills, attracted by the crying of the children, came to them, gave them her

128

teats to suck and was so gentle to them that the king's flock-master found her licking the boys with her tongue. According to the story, his name was Faustulus. He took the children to his hut and gave them to his wife Larentia to bring up.[6]

The inversion of normal human-wolf relationships marks out the mythical quality of the story. This is an unusually benign view of a wolf, focusing on milk rather than meat and on tenderness rather than ferocity. The wolf offers nourishment to the children rather than them becoming food for a savage beast and the shepherd is able to approach, without immediately killing it, the creature that most threatens his livelihood. There are also two wolves involved in the story – an animal she-wolf and a human she-wolf. The sting in the tale as commented on by Livy is his final thought about the she-wolf who actually raised them: 'Some writers think that Larentia, from her unchaste life, had got the nickname of "She-wolf" (*lupa*, 'prostitute') among the

Romulus and
Remus with the
She-wolf, 4th
century AD,
Romano-British
mosaic discovered
in Aldborough,
North Yorkshire.

shepherds, and that this was the origin of the marvellous story.' So, linked to the striking image of a fierce wild animal preserving the lives of the abandoned boys is an altogether less noble image of them being raised by an animal-like woman, although all depictions of the she-wolf suckling the young Romulus and Remus are of her in her more culturally acceptable wolf form.

Romulus and Remus seem to have spent very little time with the legendary She-wolf before they were brought back to live with fellow human beings and it could not be claimed that she actually raised them. There are, however, more recent accounts of children who spent time with wolves, were nurtured by them and became more wolf-like than human.

Many of these accounts concern cases in India, particularly in what is now Uttar Pradesh, where from the mid- to late nineteenth century British military and colonial officials investigated and published accounts of wolf-children found there. These accounts themselves were set in the context of the apparently large numbers of children carried away and killed by wolves. An official of the Geological Survey of India, for example, claimed that he had figures showing that between 1867 and 1873, in the Kingdom of Oude alone, upwards of 100 children a year were killed by them.[7] Whether or not these reported killings represented reality, such predation was certainly something that people believed to be true. The cases of children being raised by wolves was an altogether more complex phenomenon than their being killed by wolves. It involved predation, in the sense of wolves taking children away, but they were clearly not preyed on as food. Little attention is paid in the available accounts to how these children were able to survive with wolves; instead it is the human condition, or lack of it, of the children when they have been brought back to human habitation and society that is stressed.

Through a review of such cases published by Major-General Sir W. H. Sleeman in 1888, it is possible to extract key issues of what sort of creatures these wolf-children were thought to be when they began their life with humans after their wolf-like existence. The general pattern was that such children were taken at a young age (although, significantly, never as babies), usually between two and six, and so they had experienced early human socialization and enculturation before their abduction. Wolves snatched them from the fields where their parents were working or from villages when the parents were sleeping and dragged them off to the wilderness. Some authors speculated on the reasons for such abductions and why the children were raised and not simply killed. One colonial official, for example, wrote that if these stories were true he could only offer two suggestions to account for this. The first is that when the wolf returned with the child other wolves had returned to the pack with plenty of meat to feed on and therefore had no interest in killing and eating the child. He imagined that the child was allowed to lie in the den, possibly suckling on the female, although why suckling should be necessary for a fully weaned child is not considered. Eventually the human came to be treated as a family member. His other suggestion is touchingly anthropomorphic: 'Secondly, and, perhaps more probably it may be that the wolf's cubs, having been stolen, the children have been carried off to fill their places, and have been fondled and suckled.'[8]

The next stage in these stories was that people spotted children accompanying wolves and either caught them in the open or dug them out from the wolves' den and returned with them to human habitation. Sometimes parents or other relatives recognized them as children who were lost years earlier. The returned wolf-children preferred to walk on all fours, disliked clothing, preferred raw meat and bones to cooked food and, long after their return to human life, were unable to speak – although a few were able to utter some individual words. Contemporary commentators were fascinated by issues of wildness and civilization raised by these cases. In particular they focused on how the children were unable to develop and return to what they regarded as a fully human state: walking upright,

wearing clothes, eating cooked rather than raw food and, most significantly, speaking. The most written-about case concerns two Indian girls, Amala and Kamala, whom the Reverend J.A.L. Singh claimed to have rescued from a wolf's den near the village of Godamuri, west of Calcutta, in 1920. After their rescue they were looked after at Singh's orphanage but Amala died a year later and Kamala lived only until 1929. Again these two girls were represented as never re-attaining a full human condition. Although Singh published a diary about the lives of these girls in the 1920s, the case attracted worldwide attention when he, and American anthropologist Robert Zingg, published *Wolf Children and Feral Man* (1942). Subsequent analysts, particularly psychologists (for example Bruno Bettelheim) and sociologists, have used the cases of wolf-children to argue for theories of how early childhood socialization relates, or does not relate, to adult development and, particularly, whether childhood influences inevitably persist or whether they can be lost irrecoverably when separated from other humans.[9]

Such cases in India offered a setting and a context for the emergence of the most famous wolf-boy in the world – Mowgli. John Lockwood Kipling, the father of Rudyard, was certainly aware of the stories of children raised by wolves and seems to have been convinced of their veracity, probably because of the authority of the colonial officials' accounts. In an aside in his *Man and Beast in India* (1891), he comments: 'India is probably the cradle of wolf-children stories, which are here universally believed and supported by a cloud of testimony.'[10] Rudyard must also have been aware of these published accounts, or knew of them through his father, when he was writing the stories for what would become *The Jungle Book* (1894).

In the first story one of the wolves seems to know something of the stories of children raised by wolves. In 'Mowgli's

Brothers', Father Wolf and Mother Wolf hear rustling in a thicket. Father Wolf prepares to leap onto whatever is making the noise but at the moment of his attack he has to prevent himself landing on his prey when he sees that it is 'a man's cub'. Mother Wolf, who has never seen such a creature, asks for it to be brought to her:

> 'How little! How naked, and – how bold!' said Mother Wolf, softly. The baby was pushing his way between the cubs to get close to the warm hide. 'Ahai! He is taking his meal with the others. And so this is a man's cub. Now was there ever a wolf who could boast of a man's cub among her children?'
>
> 'I have heard now and again of such a thing, but never in our Pack or in my time,' said Father Wolf.[11]

Although his surrogate wolf parents protect him in infancy Mowgli never has an easy time with the wolf pack and, importantly, he is always called the 'man's cub'. He never becomes fully wolf and he is never totally of the jungle. When the cubs are a little older Father Wolf has to present them, Mowgli included, to a meeting of the full pack, under the gaze of its leader, Akela. Shere Khan the tiger demands the boy as his rightful prey (because he had attacked Mowgli's parents) and the other wolves side with him – arguing that they should have nothing to do with a man's cub. It is Baloo the bear and Bagheera the panther who speak up for the boy. Mowgli is left with Akela, Baloo, Bagheera and his immediate family of wolves, those who will teach him to be a jungle dweller.

Mowgli's life in the jungle and with the wolves of the Seeonee Pack is something of a mirror image of the puzzlement of nineteenth-century commentators on the nature of wolf-children

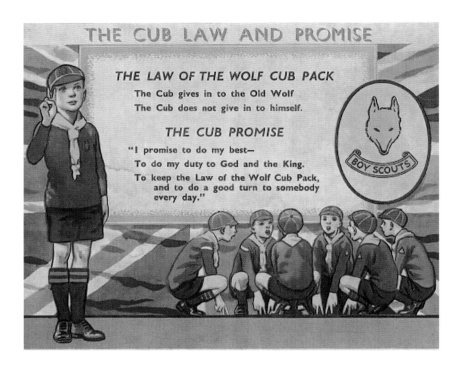

THE CUB LAW AND PROMISE

THE LAW OF THE WOLF CUB PACK

The Cub gives in to the Old Wolf
The Cub does not give in to himself.

THE CUB PROMISE

"I promise to do my best—
To do my duty to God and the King.
To keep the Law of the Wolf Cub Pack,
and to do a good turn to somebody
every day."

BOY SCOUTS

'The Cub Law and Promise', instruction poster for the UK Scout Association, mid-20th century.

when they were returned to civilization and had to live with humans. Here the animals have to try to understand what place a man's cub might have in their world and whether he has lost enough of his humanness, whether he is animal enough, and wild enough, to be one of them.

Mowgli's adventures in the Indian jungle had an enormous immediate appeal to readers that has continued through the books themselves and in the popularity of the 1967 animated Disney film. In the book, although the man's cub has a rancorous and ambiguous relationship with other wolves in the jungle, he has entirely supportive and affectionate relationships with his adoptive family and with Akela, the wise leader of the pack. It was these relationships that were celebrated through the enduring popularity of the youth movement founded in Britain during the First World War.

Robert Baden-Powell began the establishment of the Boy Scout movement with a camp for twenty boys on Brownsea Island in the south of England in 1907. He developed his thoughts for the movement in *Scouting for Boys*, published in serialized form in 1908. With the phenomenal success of the Scouts there was gradual pressure for the formation of a junior branch to allow the participation of boys younger than eleven years old. In 1916, with the publication of *The Wolf Cub's Handbook*, the Wolf Cubs came into being. Mowgli and his relationship with the wolves was the founding myth of the Wolf Cubs and was used by Baden-Powell to establish the proper relationships that a Cub should have with his Pack and with its leader Akela. Here the image of wolves was of creatures that lived in a supportive, orderly and disciplined society. They respected their leader, they were cooperative and they brought up their offspring to be good, true and loyal members of the pack. As the Law of the Wolf Cub Pack demands: 'The Cub gives in to the Old Wolf; The Cub does not give in to himself.'

For the Cubs themselves he makes an explicit connection with how young wolves are raised and taught to be members of the pack through discipline, a quality that he greatly admires in both wolves and humans. Wolf cubs are allowed to play but they must do so under the watchful eye of an adult. If a wolf cub attempts to wander off on his own his mother will soon bring him back:

Suddenly she will raise her head, and stare at the wanderer. In a moment he will stop and look at her, and an instant later will come trotting back. Nothing is said, there is no sound, but the sharp young cub understands what is wanted of him, and does it at once. That is obedience.

It is what the human Wolf Cubs might want to do, too – see what is wanted of them, and doing it without waiting to be told or ordered.

That is how wolves, when they grow up, become such good hunters. The pack works together, and obeys the order of the chief wolf.[12]

Part of Baden-Powell's view is that through disciplined play the young can be taught how to be proper adults. Wolf cubs begin to learn about serious hunting through play hunting and, by learning from the adults, they take their place in the social life of the pack. Human Wolf Cubs, through play, have their wildness and unruliness gradually channelled so that they can enter the more disciplined and demanding world of the Scout troop. Here are two worlds – the animal world of the pack and the human world of the troop – both parallel and mutually reinforcing.

Baden-Powell seemed to believe that the members of a natural wolf pack responded to the howled demands of their leader to gather together and the Grand Howl of the Wolf Cubs became a key ritual response to their leader. When Akela, the Cubmaster, entered the room or when he called 'Pack' the boys should gather around him immediately and howl.

Illustrations of wolf cub 'howling' from the *Wolf Cub Handbook*.

The global Wolf Cub movement was suffused with celebratory lupine imagery until 1967 when, in a major reform, the Wolf Cubs became Cub Scouts and the animal world of *The Jungle Book* was cast aside in favour of fuller incorporation into the modern world of the Scouts. However, the iconic image of the wolf as a wise, powerful and respected leader was not entirely lost: the emblem of the Bronze Wolf remains the highest award given to an individual who has made an exceptional contribution to the international Scouting movement.

The Boy Scouts of America was founded in 1910 and rapidly became a popular youth movement. The Wolf Cubs, however, with their *Jungle Book* founding myth, did not find a home there in the same form. The young Americans were called Cub Scouts rather than Wolf Cubs, the groups were named dens rather than packs, and they had a Scout rather than Akela as their guardian and leader. Perhaps this distancing from the original iconography resulted from the perception at the time of wolves as creatures fit only for eradication. The idea of wolves being appropriate role models for socializing young boys or creatures from which a compelling image of a human community could be modelled would have been anathema to a frontier-inspired society.

By the time the Boy Scout movement crossed the Atlantic there already existed a youth movement that emphasized an appreciation of, and an engagement with, the spaces of wilderness. In 1902 the nature writer Ernest Thompson Seton (who trapped the legendary wolf Lobo; see chapter Three) founded the League of Woodcraft Indians, later to be known simply as the Woodcraft Indians. Central to Thompson Seton's vision was the development of boys 'through the promotion of interest in out-of-door life and woodcraft, the preservation of wildlife and landscape and the promotion of good fellowship among its members'.[13] He believed that immersing boys in the world of wilderness, where they could 'discover, preserve, develop and diffuse the culture of the Redman', would act as an antidote to the debilitating effects of civilization.[14]

The movement was part of a growing concern with how people should relate to 'wilderness' as a powerfully evocative space in the American imagination and it would gradually lead to a re-evaluation of wolves. Thompson Seton's determination to offer young boys an experience of the emotional, aesthetic and practical benefits of wilderness was part of a more general concern by some Americans for a re-evaluation and rediscovery of wilderness, and with enthusing urban dwellers about something with which they had lost contact. As environmental historian Roderick Nash suggests, at the end of the nineteenth century some commentators were beginning to sense that the pioneering spirit of the frontier, which they believed had shaped the American character, was being lost and that this was related to the loss of areas of wilderness to the demands of civilization. Nash points out that before the 1890s the wilderness was the adversary of the pioneer and it was cast as 'the villain of the morality play of western expansion'.[15] However, by the end of the century some people had begun to rethink the idea and reality of wilderness and there was a view that 'without wild country the concepts of frontier and pioneer were meaningless'.[16] When Americans no longer had to advance into the unknown, nor do battle to dominate and tame wild spaces, the natural world could be valued differently.

Not only were such spaces newly responded to as places with intrinsic value but so were the beings, both human and non-human, living there. Although Native American people were far from being emancipated citizens, the emerging cult of wilderness did include a gradual, if romanticized, appreciation of their societies and cultures. Likewise there was the gradual emergence of the idea that wolves and other carnivores might have a place, and a valuable one, in the wild landscapes.

This reconsideration of the ethology and ecology of wolves was led by biologists and zoologists who took themselves off to wild places in an attempt to understand the actuality, rather than the cultural construction, of wolf life and behaviour. The beginnings of the systematic investigation of wolf ecology can be traced to the work of Sigurd Olson.[17] He conducted field research of his own but also worked with material collected by wolf trappers in an attempt to sort, as he saw it, fact from fiction regarding wolf social organization. He published this first scientific material on pack size, social organization and range in journal articles in 1938. From 1939 until 1941 Adolph Murie conducted fieldwork with wolves in Mount McKinley National Park, Alaska (now named the Denali National Park and Preserve), that was to result in the publication of the ground-breaking and enormously influential work *The Wolves of Mount McKinley* (1944). During this time he observed wolves closely, studied their hunting, analysed their faeces to determine their sources of food and examined the remains of wolf kills to see if there was anything significant about the animals that had been preyed on.

Murie was not, at the time, a passionate advocate for all wolves and in the foreword to his study he understood that wolves had to be killed when their activities clashed with human interests:

The wolf is a powerful animal, and a cunning one, and unfortunately has run counter to the economic interests of man in settled regions. The war against the wolf on our western plains, when cattle replaced the buffalo and the wolf became a serious menace to the livestock industry, is an interesting phase in early western history. It was, of course, necessary that the wolf should go from those regions.[18]

He suggests, however, that people might want to retain wolves somewhere in North America and national parks might be a good place:

In considering the wolf and the general ecological picture in Mount McKinley National Park it must be emphasized that national parks are a specialized type of land use. Wildlife policies suitable to national parks – areas dedicated to preserving samples of primitive America – obviously may differ from those applicable to lands devoted to other uses.[19]

A further suggestion, that the authorities of national parks should have a good scientific knowledge of the issues they were dealing with before they began interfering and attempting to manage wild animals, was to be of fundamental importance for wolves. In North America researchers began to work at acquiring that scientific knowledge. Wolf specialists such as Milt Stenlund, Durward Allen, Doug Pimlott, Rolf Peterson and later the doyen of wolf studies, David Mech, followed Murie's pioneering work by studying wolves in the wild. Their painstakingly assembled material, which revealed the complexities of wolf lives and how they interacted with their environments, persuaded many to reconsider the wolf as an essential and integral part of the landscapes it inhabited and the ecological systems in which it was now seen to play a role. At the beginning of the twentieth century the wolf was an animal known only from anecdote; by the end of the century it was one of the most written-about land mammals in the world.[20]

Alongside the scientific re-evaluation of the wolf and an appreciation of its place in the wild there also developed a popular cultural re-evaluation. The image of a feared and demonic creature gradually gave way to one that captured the newly celebratory spirit that animated the wild and the wilderness. The wolf did not have to change its behaviour to bring about a change of image but its behaviour and motivations had to be reassessed, and a social and cultural space had to open up in which this newly charismatic creature could exist. The changing popular attitudes to the wolf were gradual, complex and multi-faceted. Unlike the development of scientific work on the wolf, they cannot be pinned down precisely. For many, however, one passage has become emblematic of the revelation of a new, true spirit of the wolf; and that religious image of revelation is not far-fetched. Aldo Leopold, the pioneer environmentalist and wilderness philosopher who advanced the idea of 'the land ethic', achieved posthumous worldwide acclaim for *A Sand County Almanac* (1949), which became a classic of environmental litera-ture. Leopold began his career as a forester with the United States Forestry Service. Although he was always a keen conservationist, his early notion of conservation was underpinned by the need to dominate and manage. Central to this domination and manage-ment was the killing of predators, particularly wolves, and Leopold killed plenty of them. He was an active member of the campaign to eradicate wolves from the cattle ranges and deer territories of the southwestern states, for example. In 1920, in an address to a national game conference, he argued that: 'It's going to take a lot of patience and money to catch the wolf . . . in New Mexico, but the last one must be caught before the job can be fully successful.'[21] However, in 1944 he had an experience that profoundly changed his philosophy of wilderness; his pub-lished account of that experience had a significant influence in reshaping many people's views on practices of wolf killing.

Leopold and his colleagues were eating lunch when they saw what they thought was a doe crossing the river beneath them. When the creature emerged from the water they saw it was a wolf that was quickly enveloped in 'a welcoming mêlée of wag-ging tails and playful maulings'. But this was not a sight to be savoured and enjoyed:

In those days we never heard of passing up a chance to kill a wolf. In a second we were pumping lead into the pack, but with more excitement than accuracy: how to aim a steep downhill shot is always confusing. When our rifles were empty, the old wolf was down, and a pup was dragging a leg into impassable slide-rocks.

We reached the old wolf in time to watch a fierce green fire dying in her eyes. I realized then, and I have known ever since, that there was something new to me in those eyes – something known only to her and the mountain.[22]

This was a Damascene conversion, albeit in reverse. Saul, the killer of Christians, on the road to Damascus to continue his killing, was blinded by the light of God and hears the voice of Jesus asking him 'why persecutest thou me' (Acts 22:6). This was the moment of his conversion – he was blinded but he could see. As the wolf's eyes become blind to the world, Leopold's were opened and he knew that he had to stop his own persecution of wolves and to speak out against that persecution by others. This powerful and often quoted description of the moment of realization of an unnecessary, senseless and now morally, emotionally and ecologically wrong killing came to have an enormous impact in North America and across the world.

Although Leopold's plea for the place of wolves in the wilderness had a strong element of emotional and ethical concern, it was also based on sound scientific study. Another landmark plea for wolves supposedly began as a scientific study but ended as a vehement attack on animal scientists and the management of wolves. In 1948–9, about the time of the publication of Leopold's book, Farley Mowat, a naturalist with powerful storytelling skills, was employed by the Dominion Wildlife Service of Canada to undertake an observational study of the relations between wolves and caribou in the far north of the country. Soon after his encounter with what he called the Wolf House Pack, Mowat quickly shed what little scientific interest and ethos he had in favour of inserting himself into the life of the pack, which he recounted in emotional, subjective terms in *Never Cry Wolf* (1963).

In terms of the descriptions of the lives of wolves this was more an intensely anthropomorphic soap opera than an account of the social ecology of a wolf pack. Mowat's story revolves around a small wolf pack consisting of George and Angelina, the breeding pair, their un-named offspring, and a pup-sitting male named Uncle Albert. George is described as massive, eminently regal, 'with an air of masterful certainty' and 'affectionate within reasonable bounds'. The female is 'beautiful, ebullient, passionate to a degree, and devilish when the mood was on her'.[23] The life of this pack was, as Mowat describes it, joyful and idyllic. They were a supportive family that hunted together and shared food, and the playful pups were treated with indulgence. This was not the sort of wolf lives that had been described before.

What was also novel was Mowat's account of his life with the pack. The wolves were at first nervous and curious, although never threatening, in his presence and soon he seemed to be tolerated as an outsider who was able to sit closely to observe them and even allowed to follow them on their hunting trips. This was something even more powerfully novel – a human living among wolves with no fear of attack. Mowat knew that his claims would be dismissed as unscientific and throughout the book he lambasts and lampoons 'Homobiologist' as an idiot who had never got close enough, and was not imaginative enough, to understand the lives of these creatures. He was interested in imagining and creating a different set of truths about wolves from those of the scientists and he set out to communicate this through emotion and empathy rather than apparently objective science. As he commented in the preface to a later edition, 'it is my practice never to allow facts to interfere with the truth'.[24]

Never Cry Wolf provoked powerful storms of reaction – both scientific and popular – and, despite the reason and science of the former, it was the emotion of the latter that was to prevail. The book, translated into more than twenty languages, is still hugely popular after nearly 50 years in print.[25] As Mowat expected, the wolf scientists returned fire, lampooning him in turn as 'Hardly Knowit' and attacking him for having produced a work of fiction about wolf lives that bore no relation to reality. Despite this criticism the book had an important impact on the general public.

As a result of its publication the Canadian Wildlife Service received mail from all over the world condemning its programmes of intense wolf culling and supporting the man who was seen as a champion of these wild creatures in the face of an unfeeling wildlife bureaucracy. Mowat's account of wolf lives clearly resonated with large sections of the public and his version of how it was to be a wolf had more credibility for them than did the versions of the scientists. As Karen Jones observes: 'Derided by the scientific establishment, Mowat's fable instead became a narrative of environmental truth in North American culture.'[26] This was a fable for a new age and, in important ways, a founding fable of that age. George, Angeline and their offspring were newly conceived wolves, emblematic of the dangers posed to the innocent creatures of the wilderness by ravening humans. Any evil and savagery now existed in the minds and actions of humans rather than in the spirit and behaviour of wolves. David Mech, while warning against reading the book as a realistic rather than a fictional account of the lives of wolves, did suggest that some good had come from it: 'It has served to

stir the public from its apathy to the plight of the wolf. In this sense it offsets the effects of the classic "Little Red Riding Hood".[27] The continuing popularity of Mowat's northern adventures and the possibility of humans living in harmony with wolves were both enhanced by the release by Disney of the film *Never Cry Wolf* (1983) based on the story. This tapped into the growing popular imagining of wolves as unthreatening and essential components of the wild.

Mowat, at least in print, seemed not to have been influenced by or interested in the growing scientific literature available but there soon emerged a highly influential new fictional account of an intersection of human and wolf lives, based on some of the best of scientific writing. In 1972 Jean Craighead George, a respected writer of children's literature and a keen natural historian, published *Julie of the Wolves*, the first of a trilogy. At the heart of the books is the relationship of a girl (named Miyax when she is her Inupiat self and Julie when she is between Inupiat and Anglo cultures) with a pack of wolves. At the beginning of *Julie of the Wolves* she is lost and almost starving on the tundra when she comes upon them. She knows from her Inupiat hunter father, Kapugen, that humans could communicate with wolves and that wolves would provide food for humans if they were asked in a proper manner. Through Miyax's attempt to make contact with them and her gradual incorporation into the pack, the author is able to reveal to the reader the intricacies of wolf communication, the wolves' world of hierarchy, hunting, mate selection, breeding, the rearing of pups and the organization and protection of territories and also the dangers the wolves face from the humans who seek to protect their interests from these wild hunters. In the first book of the trilogy the lives of the pack are recounted from Miyax's point of view as she forms her relationship with them. In the last book the perspective is reversed and the reader is offered an account from within the pack, the wolves' perspective on their lives in which the girl features as someone who now lives a human life but who is an occasional and warmly welcomed guest in their world.

Although this richly evocative account of wolf lives is highly anthropomorphized it is crafted out of close reading of wolf biology and ethology. Indeed it was the new ethological knowledge that prompted Craighead George to begin the trilogy. From Mech's work on the wolves of Isle Royale she picked up on the 'friendliness' among wolves and describes how in a flight with Mech over wolf territory she saw 'the father wolf coming home and the pups running to meet him just like kids in suburbia'.[28] Craighead George paid close attention to the work of other wolf researchers on the issues of attachment and hierarchy in wolf packs and later she followed the reintroduction of wolves to Yellowstone Park, to which she returned each year to experience this wolf environment.

Craighead George's wolves might be named and given personal characteristics but these are biological wolves presented in a literary style, a very different shift in perspective from previous representations of wolves based on human fears and hatreds. Just as adult fears of wolves were, for centuries, transposed into the big bad wolves of stories for children, so contemporary adult re-evaluations of and admiration for wolves saw them represented in a new light in children's literature such that they are no longer terrifying creatures.[29] Many writers of children's literature have refashioned the image of wolves as part of their concern for environmental and ecological issues: they have written about how wolves live their lives; they have given wolf characters a voice to explain why they have been maligned and misunderstood; they have re-evoked them in mythical and mystical forms in historical and fantasy stories; and they have retold stories of the big bad wolf so that the wolf becomes the hero rather than the villain.[30]

A particularly delightful reworking of the story of the wolf who terrorizes the three little pigs in their houses of straw, wood and stone is *Eco-Wolf and the Three Pigs*.[31] In this tale the wolf is a young, punk-hippy eco-warrior fighting the three pigs, who are representatives of Pigsty Properties, builders of luxury homes across his beautiful valley. The pigs care nothing for the environment: they destroy old oak trees for the frame of their straw house and gouge out the land, destroying rabbit burrows and cutting down trees to build their wooden house with its six bedrooms, garage, swimming pool and drive. The animals of the valley manage to destroy these houses but they seem defeated by a high-rise tower block built on top of a shopping centre and surrounded by roads. Eco-Wolf makes a sit-in protest at the top of the power station they have constructed and he uses his wigwam to send the smoke back down the chimney. In a reversal of the traditional story, one of the pigs tries to climb up inside the chimney to get the wolf but he becomes stuck, the pressure builds up and the power station and the entire town explode. As an act of retribution the pigs are made to clean up the valley and dig new homes for the evicted rabbits before they finally leave the valley in the capable hands of Eco-Wolf. In this and other wolf stories for children there is a conflation, translation and reconfiguration of fairy tales and environmental ideas figured in the species that has been the focus and the victim of both.

Other modern children's books do not seek to set out a message but rather play with key elements of well-known wolf stories. *The Wolf Who Cried Boy* is a delicious and lightly gruesome story of this kind. Little Wolf is tired of the traditional wolf food – 'They stole sheep, ran after rabbits and dined on ducklings and deer' – that his mother serves. What Little Wolf wants

ANIMAL FIGURE OR SIMILAR ARTICLE

Filed Dec. 30, 1933

Walt Disney, copy of an early patent sketch of the 'Big Bad Wolf', 1934.

Inventor

Walter E. Disney

By *Lyon + Lyon* :

Attorneys

is to eat Boy and he demands to know why he can't. Father Wolf reflects nostalgically that, 'there was a time when a clever wolf could snatch a shepherd boy off a hill or pluck a farm boy out of a field. Why, there was nothing better than a steaming plate of boy chops.' He tells his son that if he ever sees a boy then he and his mother would be happy to catch him and cook him. Next day Little Wolf pretends to see one and runs home howling 'Boy!' His parents set out in excited pursuit but find nothing. The evening meal of Three-Pig Salad is ruined, 'The bricks are limp, the straw is damp and the sticks have turned all . . . sticky.'

To Little Wolf's delight they have to have snacks. The next day he pulls the same trick and again dinner is ruined because the apples in the Granny Smith Pie are mushy and 'Granny's gone all crusty and hard.' Snacks again. But his parents are onto his tricks and are determined not to respond. The next day Little Wolf not only sees a boy, he sees an entire pack of them: Wolf Cubs in full uniform marching behind a wolf banner. Despite his excited shouting and pleading Little Wolf is ignored. Even when one of the Wolf Cubs ventures into the cave and eats Little Wolf's crisps, they still will not believe him. He is forced back to appreciating traditional food. He continues to imagine the delights of cooked boy but he never cries 'Boy!' again.[32]

But it is not just in children's literature that a revision of the wolf can be found. From the latter part of the twentieth century writers for adults also celebrated wolves and the alluring nature of wolfish qualities that they believed should be embraced rather than feared. This discovery and celebration was particularly potent and influential in the work of two feminist writers – Angela Carter and Clarissa Pinkola Estés – but the wolves they created and the qualities they admired were not based on the wolves of the biologists but rather on inverted and subverted stereotypes of the dangerous, male, wolfish ways of myth and fable. Chapter Two above was introduced with a quotation from Carter apparently warning the reader of the dangers of the wolf, but the main character of her short story 'The Company of Wolves', a Red Riding Hood figure, neither fears nor flees the wolf who waits for her. This encounter is one of liberation and self-realization, rather than a threat to her civilized self. When the wolf says he will eat her she laughs for 'she knew that she was nobody's meat'. As in the fable for children she undresses and burns her clothes, but in this modern fable she also undresses the wolf/werewolf and kisses him while 'Every wolf in the world now howled a prothalamion outside the window.' Here the howling, an aural image of threat and danger, is converted into a song in celebration of a forthcoming wedding. Unlike Red Riding Hood, the girl does not succumb to a predator but willingly embraces, quite literally, the creature's wolfish power. Sexual violence is converted into sexual satisfaction – after which, 'sweet and sound she sleeps in granny's bed, between the paws of the tender wolf'.[33]

While Carter's heroine literally embraces the wild through a relationship with the wolf, Pinkola Estés, a Jungian psychoanalyst, poet and storyteller, wants women to celebrate the wild within, which she connects with the spirit of the wolf. Here it is the female wolf that is the centre of celebration. Women, like wolves, have been punished and persecuted for what others have perceived as their dangerous and threatening natures but for Pinkola Estés it is time for women to reverse this and to connect with this spirit, to run with wolves and not from them and all they have represented:

Aristocrats transformed into wolves. Still from the wedding scene in *The Company of Wolves* (dir. Neil Jordan, 1984), a film based on the short story of the same name by Angela Carter.

Healthy wolves and healthy women share certain psychic characteristics: keen sensing, playful spirit, and a heightened capacity for devotion. Wolves and women are relational by nature, inquiring, possessed of great endurance and strength. They are deeply intuitive, intensely concerned with their young, their mates and their pack. They are experienced in adapting to constantly changing circumstances; they are fiercely stalwart and very brave.[34]

It is highly significant that Pinkola Estés chooses the wolf, rather than any other creature, to link women and the spirit of the wild. No other creature of the American wilderness has the cultural history of denigratory representations that she, like Carter, needs to subvert in order to create a newly imagined wild. It is only the power of the wolf's demonized stereotype that allows her, in a radical shift of perspective, to use the wolf as an image of the salvatory powers of the wild. It is only because the wolf has been persecuted that it is a suitable image for freedom. As she comments, both wolves and women

have been hounded, harassed, and falsely imputed to be devouring and devious, overly aggressive, of less value than those who are their detractors. They have been the targets of those who would clean up the wilds as well as the wildish environs of the psyche, extincting the instinctual, and leave no trace of it behind. The predation of wolves and women by those who misunderstand them is strikingly similar.[35]

In earlier periods of history (as shown in chapter Two) partaking of, or being possessed by, a dangerous and destructive wolfish spirit was something that demanded punishment and even execution. Now the spirit that governs the wolf is desired and embraced as a means of reconnecting people with their animal, wild nature.

It is also significant that at the beginning of the book Pinkola Estés offers the reader her creation 'La Loba' (The female Wolf), an essentialized wild, wise witch woman, to connect wolves and women in a new way. La Loba searches through the countryside for wolf bones until she assembles a complete wolf skeleton. She sings over the skeleton and her singing brings about a fully fleshed wolf. With further singing it becomes alive, breathes, runs off and 'is suddenly transformed into a laughing woman who runs free toward the horizon'.[36] With La Loba the author seems to be suggesting a link to the perception of wolves and a nature that indigenous peoples connected with in North America before the later colonizing cultures arrived.

Just as running with wolves became a potent image for women connecting with idealized wolves, so the image of dancing with wolves became one of different human cultures connecting through an engagement with a wolf. In the film of *Dances With Wolves* (1990), John Dunbar, a young cavalry lieutenant, is left alone in Fort Sedgewick, an army outpost in 1863, as he journeys away from his militarized, Anglo world into the world of the local Comanche people, in which he becomes immersed and fully at home. In Michael Blake's original novel of the same name, Dunbar's relationship with a wolf is used to mark his transition from one culture to another.

When the wolf first appears at the fort, Dunbar's instinct is to fire shots to frighten it away but he realizes that the creature is motivated by nothing more than curiosity and he leaves it be; this marks him as an unusual Anglo. When the wolf next appears, as he rides across the plain, he knows that it is not threatening and is comfortable with its presence at a distance as it keeps pace with him during the ride. The main theme of the book is Dunbar's slowly developing relationship with the nearby Comanche but alongside this, keeping pace with it and indicating it, is his developing relationship with the wolf. With both the wolf and the Comanche the gulf between them is closed. In the case of the wolf it culminates in the creature coming into the fort and lying close to Dunbar. The moment is highly significant – wilderness comes into civilization but that civilization, the much neglected fort, is slowly collapsing, as is Dunbar's relationship with it. He no longer feels at home there and gradually leaves his civilization for a culture in the wilderness that he had previously been taught was uncivilized. As the wolf gradually comes in from the outside, so too does Dunbar in relation to the world of the Comanche.

Not only do the man and wolf come physically close, they also share food. Dunbar leaves out meat for the wolf and the wolf brings a freshly killed prairie chicken to him. On one occasion Dunbar throws a piece of bacon to the wolf, which picks it up and trots off with it. This act is observed by Kicking Bird, one of the Comanche, who has been trying to puzzle out what sort of creature this unusual white man is. As a result of this simple act Dunbar and Kicking Bird literally connect. Dunbar recounts the story in his journal:

> To me it was a happy event and nothing more. But the quiet one [Kicking Bird] seemed unduly affected by the display. When I turned back to him, his face seemed more peaceful than ever. He nodded at me several times, then walked up and put his hand on my shoulder as though he approved.[37]

It is through his relationship with a wild wolf that Kicking Bird and his companions begin to relate to Dunbar, not as a representative of the enemy but as a potential member of their culture and community, which they mark by giving him a Comanche name.

On a trip to the Comanche camp Dunbar is followed by the wolf and he tries to shoo it away verbally. The wolf keeps

A 'new age' – two imagined spirits of the wild come together, 1999, postcard by Meiklejohn Graphics.

following. Dunbar dismounts and attempts to chase it away; the wolf runs away but then bounds back; Dunbar chases it again and pulls its tail; the wolf retreats but just when Dunbar thinks he has succeeded, the wolf sneaks back and nips his ankle. All of this romping has been witnessed with great amusement by a group of Comanche:

> Kicking Bird also knew that he had witnessed something precious, something that had provided a solution to one of the puzzles surrounding the white man . . . the puzzle of what to call him.
>
> A man should have a real name . . . particularly when it is a white who acts like this one.
>
> He felt certain that this was the right one. It suited the white soldier's personality. People would remember him by this. And Kicking Bird himself, with two witnesses to back him up, had been present at the time the Great Spirit revealed it.
>
> He said it to himself several times as he came down the slope. The sound of it was as good as the name itself.
>
> Dances with Wolves.[38]

In an important sense the representations of Dunbar's relationship with the wolf capture, and only make sense in terms of, a late twentieth-century revaluing and re-imagining of wolves. Although set in the nineteenth century, it is unlikely that a novelist of that period would have expressed such sympathetic views of wolves in relation to indigenous cultures. For a white man, and even more for a soldier representing an army responsible for controlling and killing what were perceived as wild peoples, to lose his name and culture and be renamed after a wild animal by such people would have been unthinkable. Whereas the nineteenth century linked indigenous peoples with wolves in terms of their essentially savage, civilization-threatening natures, during the twentieth century the linkage came to be one of a wolf spirit and an Indian spirit, both of which were represented in mystical, idealized and nostalgic ways as being in harmony with and emblematic of the natural world – the wild – which had been lost to a destructive civilization and should now be recovered. In these representations, usually romanticized and sentimentalized, both the wolf and the Indian became essentialized in highly condensed symbols created by people who found in, and imposed on, the creatures and the peoples a focus for a new spiritual longing.

At present the wolf is, for many people, a charismatic creature in the sense of possessing an aura and having a capacity to inspire devotion and enthusiasm. The wolf now carries the cultural weight of being emblematic of the wilderness, a necessary physical and spiritual antidote to modern material civilization and a symbol of the well-being of that wilderness. If wolves are there then the wilderness is truly alive. Once again, as with the case of the reworking of the image of wolves in fiction, this creation of the spiritualized, charismatic wolf has depended on the demonized wolf of previous centuries and at its heart there is a sense of an attempt to atone for the persecution of wolves by protecting them, reintroducing them and celebrating their presence; it is a form of reparation to the species and to the wilderness.

This keen interest in wolves has been marked by a huge growth of popular natural history and photographic books with titles such as *The Great American Wolf*, *The Company of Wolves*, *Wolf Songs*, *Wolf: Spirit of the Wild* and *The Wolf Almanac: A Celebration of Wolves and their Lives*. As well as a thriving literary market for

stories of wolves, there is also a huge market for images and representations of them in other forms, which seems to indicate a radical shift from wolf hatred to wolf love. Whereas creatures surrounding and threatening homes was once a common image of the fear of wolves, they, or at least their representations, are now welcomed into homes by people who are seemingly keen to surround themselves with them. A trawl through eBay and other online sales sites finds hundreds of wolves on posters, photographs and paintings; calendars; jewellery and clothing; bedspreads, blankets and rugs; cups, mugs and plates and on a whole range of household decorations. The creature that for a long time was regarded as base and without value has been newly commodified and has had an economic value imposed on it, or at least on its image and representations. People can even take a step beyond representations and purchase a living wolf. Specialist breeders offer purebred wolf pups for sale as pets and many more offer wolf-dog hybrids. Alongside this trade, many websites and discussion groups celebrate the pleasures

The 'spirituality' of wilderness, 1999, postcard by Meiklejohn Graphics.

HUNT · SUSI · KRIIMSILM · VÕSAVILLEM · HALLIVATIMEES · PÜHA JÜRI KUTSIKAS

Post Office First Day cover, Estonia, 2004.

of owning and living with such creatures. Others set out to warn of the difficulties and dangers they might be creating and the discomfort and distress for the animals concerned in this inappropriate process of bringing the wild into the home or the breeding of the wild with the domesticated.

Recently the wolf has even been revalued musically. In 1936 Sergei Prokofiev was commissioned by the Central Children's Theatre in Moscow to write a piece to teach children about the instruments of the orchestra. He wrote a story of a valiant, although disobedient, boy who captures a wolf that has eaten a family duck. At the end of the story Peter, with his grandfather and local hunters, proudly leads the wolf to captivity in a local zoo. *Peter and the Wolf* is the most widely known musical rendition of a wolf, a rather un-terrifying wolf but still one that must be punished for its predation. The promotion of a new Russian wolf, but one that was created to have an international resonance, emerged in the early 2000s with a reworking of *Peter and the Wolf*. The Russian National Orchestra commissioned *Wolf Tracks*, premiered in 2002, from the French composer Jean-Pascal Beintus and the American writer Walter Kraemer. In this piece the grandfather is now Peter in old age who remembers his part in the *Peter and the Wolf* that his grandson,

Peter, is now reading. Young Peter wants adventure and wants to capture a wolf, but this time the grandfather does not warn him of the dangers of wolves but instead tells him that, with their forests nearly gone, wolves are now poor and desperate creatures and that he should 'leave these noble creatures in peace'. While his grandfather sleeps, Peter sets out and finds a thin and hungry wolf that he captures in his cape. However, his triumphal return is interrupted by the wolf's whimpering and mournful howling. Peter looks into its eyes and thinks of the ruined habitat he has just run through. He realizes the wisdom of his grandfather's words and releases his wolf to return to its family. The narrator comments, 'But wait . . . *His* Wolf? It wasn't really *Peter's* wolf at all. Wolves belong to the world . . .

Erna Voigt, front cover illustration depicting Peter leading the wolf into captivity, from Sergei Prokofiev's *Peter and the Wolf*, 1980.

163

their world, our world of wonder, of nature's splendor.' The commissioning orchestra is clear about its intention with this piece – 'a tale that converts the image of the wolf from a fearsome creature to one that represents the imperative to cherish and protect natural resources'.[39]

Modern wolf love seems as powerful as older hatreds and fears. An Internet search for 'wolves' will reveal scores of sites, such as of Defenders of Wildlife, promoting the appreciation of wolves and dedicated to dispelling older attitudes to wolves and attacking what they see as the last, wrong-headed bastions of wolf hatred. Others are educational and attempt to synthesize modern scientific knowledge; a fine example would be the site Wolf Song of Alaska.

Promoters of such understanding have also made use of digital technology. Wolfquest is a virtual version of Yellowstone National Park and its wolves. Players entering this world become wolves and learn about their environment, how to hunt and what it is like to live in a pack, to encounter other wolves and other predators, to find a mate and to raise pups. Launched in 2007 with support from a National Science Foundation grant and with biological expertise on the website provided by the Minnesota Zoo and the International Wolf Center, the free game is designed to develop a sympathetic understanding of wolves and to promote an awareness of the relations of real wolves and their habitat. Clearly many are open to its aims because the game has been downloaded some 400,000 times in 200 countries and the online discussion forum has 150,000 registered users, who together have made more than one million posts.[40]

The new devotees of lupophilia are not simply interested in reading about wolves but also want to experience them in the wild. In North America and Europe there are avid wolf watchers

in national parks (the website of Yellowstone Park updates visitors on areas where there is the highest probability of seeing wolves) and other wild spaces, and specialist travel agents organize guided tours specifically to see wolves. But seeing creatures as elusive as wolves in the wild demands skill, patience and considerable luck, and the watchers have to be prepared to return without their desired experience. For those who are not able or prepared to spend time waiting and watching in wild places, enterprising organizations, recognizing the desire and demand to be close to wolves, have established places in which such an encounter is guaranteed. There are now wolf parks, wolf havens, wolf sanctuaries, wolf centres and wolf preserves where people can see wolves up close, learn about them, watch them being fed and, in some cases, for a substantial fee, be allowed into the enclosures for what are often sold as 'unique photographic opportunities'.[41]

Frontier Airlines celebrate the wolf as 'The Spirit of the West'.

But seeing is not everything. Even when wolves were invisible to them, as they always have been most of the time, people

166

have heard their presence. For millennia the howling of wolves has been perhaps the most evocative sound of any wild creature. The human response has never been neutral: wolf howls have never simply been background sounds of the wild, the sound of creatures out there, communicating among themselves and getting on with their own lives. The howl of the lone wolf or, more powerfully, the interlaced howls of a pack has always evoked a response and the changing nature of those responses is a revealing indication of the modern triumph of lupophilia over lupophobia. In earlier periods the howling of wolves evoked a fear of dangerous and threatening creatures. The sound of wolves was a fearful, wild, savage cacophony – hair-raising cries from which people wanted to hide and protect themselves. As Peter Coates comments: 'On hearing the wolf's howl in western North America for the first time, many nineteenth-century Euro-American explorers and travelers interpreted it as sorrowful at best and frightful, devilish, and utterly otherworldly at worst.'[42] The wolf specialist Stanley Young offers the following response as being typical of those with whom he spoke about wolf howling: 'The cry of the lobo is entirely unlike that made by any other living creature; it is a prolonged, deep, wailing howl, and perhaps the most dismal sound ever heard by human ear.'[43] That same howling, once a dismal sound, is now something that people seek out. Fans of wolves can now purchase CDs that offer a wide range of wolf howls or have howling carefully augmented and mixed with the songs, chants and music of Native American cultures to form a synthesis of animal and human musicality, of the harmony of people with nature. One CD, using orchestral instruments, titled *Relax With Sounds of Wolves Enhanced with Music*, invites the listener to: 'Imagine yourself walking in the serene and unspoiled beauty of the Woods and listening to the sounds of the Wolves after a stressful day. Listen to the symphony of nature while you relax and escape into a world of natural beauty.' This association of the sounds of wolves with relaxation is something which earlier generations would have found unimaginable. Walking in the woods with wolves was certainly an experience to be declined, but fans of wolf sounds now flock in their thousands to live performances of howling. Many of the wolf parks open to visitors offer wolf-howling sessions in which those who work with the captive animals howl to them to elicit a response. In some places visitors themselves are offered the opportunity to howl or, as many places put it, 'connect and communicate' with wolves.

In 1963 the authorities of Algonquin Provincial Park, Ontario, offered the first evening of listening to wolves as part of their educational and interpretive programme. Wolf researchers had discovered that if they became skilled howlers they could provoke a response from packs and use this as a technique for locating and following them. They also realized that the responses of wolves could be used for educational and entertainment purposes. An evening of listening to wolves consisted of assembling people in the early evening along roads close to where the rangers thought wolves had been earlier that day or the day before. The specialist howlers would call and, with luck, if they were close by, the pack would respond. At first about 600 people would attend at a time; now the attendance on any one evening can be more than 2,000. The park authorities have estimated that over 126,000 people have come, not to see wolves but simply to hear them. Commenting on the success of the first events, the noted wolf researcher Ben Pimlott wrote:

> Almost inevitably the silence that follows the end of the howling pack is suddenly broken by the intense babble of the voices of people all talking together, excitedly sharing

the thrill of superb wilderness experience. Almost inevitably, too, disinterest fades and people begin to understand why man should always be prepared to share his environment with creatures of nature.[44]

From the perspectives of wolves, their howling has never been anything other than highly complex communication within and between packs. It has never been intended for ears other than wolves' and it is unlikely ever to have been produced to signal their intention towards humans, to provoke fear in them or to communicate with them. But, heard by humans, it has always been a highly charged sound. Once the fearful and baleful cacophony was the troubling sound of a wilderness

Anon., howling wolf, 1989, Russian *ex libris* plate, pen and ink drawing.

that was all too close. Now this most iconic call of the wild has become harmonic, a music of the wild that people thrill to rather than tremble at. It is one that they wish to provoke and feel they have the privilege of hearing, one that draws them imaginatively, emotionally and aesthetically into a lupophilic world of wolves.

5 Rewilding

All through the valley, the people are whispering:
The wolves are returning,
Returning to the narrow edge of our fields, our dreams.[1]
Anita Endrezze, 'Return of the Wolves'

Here, Anita Endrezze, a part-Yaqui poet, seems to welcome the return of wolves to places from which they have been eradicated by direct human action or through general human impingement on their environment. While some speak with joy of this return, others express anger that, after having waged a successful campaign against them, wolves are now being imposed on them. For them this is not something of their dreams but a nightmare.

At the beginning of the twenty-first century the wolf is still a creature of conflict, generating passionate responses for and against, and wolf wars continue to be fought. Whereas previous wars have been fought by humans directly *against* the wolf, the new wars are fought *over* the wolf in a range of campaigns and on different eco-political fronts. Two key battlegrounds are those of natural recolonization or repopulation by wolves and their deliberate reintroduction in areas from which they had previously been eradicated.

For those who are pro-wolf, the reappearance of wolves in areas where they have not been seen for generations, or even centuries, through recolonization and reintroduction is to be celebrated and supported as a return of wolves to their natural home. Those who are anti-wolf certainly do not want to extend any sort of welcome to wolves. Their responses tend to be of

The organization
'Mission: Wolf'
advocating for
the wolf in
a magazine
advertisement,
1999.

172

COLD, WINTER WINDS
ARE NOT ENOUGH TO PENETRATE
THE WOLF'S THICK COAT.

IF ONLY THE SAME WERE TRUE OF BULLETS.

Nearly 200 years ago, more than half a million gray wolves roamed North America. Today, that number has plummeted to less than 12,000. But with your help, places like Mission: Wolf can continue their efforts to ensure the gray wolf's greatest struggle for survival is natural, not man-made. Please write Mission: Wolf at P.O. Box 211, Silver Cliff, CO 81249 or call (719) 746-2919.

Mission: Wolf

two kinds. In areas of natural re-colonization local people, especially those whose livelihood depends on livestock, often express anxiety because they are neither accustomed, nor have the skills or means, to protect their animals from wolf predation and become angry with ineffective compensation schemes for animals killed. They also express anger that life is made more difficult for them by the presence of wolves that are usually legally protected, so making it an offence to kill them. They feel that wolves are permitted to be there only for the benefit, in some barely understood way, of others, usually those living in distant cities. Organized reintroductions tend to provoke stronger emotions in those who are anti-wolf and give rise to vociferous campaigns to prevent such projects. Whereas re-colonizations might be unwanted and unfortunate, at least they are natural. Reintroductions, however, supported and financed by substantial payments from local and national governmental departments or by outside conservation agencies, are seen as wilfully unnatural and unacceptable impositions by outsiders on locals. For those in favour of the reintroduction of wolves to wild places this is part of a process of righting a previous wrong done to both the species and to the wild. For opponents of such processes, however, it signifies the return of an unwanted killer, aided and supported by those who do not know, or do not care, what they are unleashing back into the world.

The most famous such battle concerned plans for the reintroduction of wolves to Yellowstone National Park. It exemplifies the complexities that can be created by the apparently simple attempt to put wolves back into places where it might be thought there would be space for them. This case begins with eradication. In their early years National Parks were not havens for all wildlife; predators had no place in the carefully managed ecosystems, and by 1925 or 1926 the last wolves in Yellowstone had been killed by government employees. In 1973 the Endangered Species Act became law and the grey wolf was the first animal to become, officially, an endangered species. With this recognition of its status the government was obliged to attempt to increase their numbers and restore them in wilderness areas. Part of this requirement saw the formation of the Rocky Mountain Wolf Recovery Team in 1975. Its initial plan, produced in 1980, failed because the complexities of the process had not been thought through. These were not so much those associated with the relationships of wolves with particular ecosystems but rather with the powers of different human vested interests and the conflicts between them. As in the long history of human–wolf relations, the central focus and concern was that of killing. This is part of a wolf's natural behaviour, but what and where they are allowed to kill has always determined whether and where they are allowed to live. In all wolf reintroduction programmes the concern has always been with whether they will kill domestic livestock, decimate particular local wildlife, or attack people. Whether people would have the right to kill wolves if their interests clashed has also always been a concern.

The Yellowstone case has been carefully documented by Hank Fischer in *Wolf Wars* (2003) and by Tom McNamee in *The Return of Wolves to Yellowstone* (1997), both of whom played significant roles in supporting the campaign to bring wolves back to the park. Both accounts document how the development of recovery plans was not simply a matter of establishing, in biological and ecological terms, whether the ecosystem of Yellowstone could sustain wolves and whether wolves could survive there. They had also to confront the issue of whether wolves ought to be *allowed* to live there – a question of biopolitics rather than biology. For all those involved, this was not a question of discussing, in a neutral manner, issues such as the potential impact of new predators on prey populations, the carrying capacity of the ecosystem, or the sustainability of wolf populations. Rather it was an impassioned campaign for or against wolves themselves that involved conflicts between a wide range of interested parties: wolf biologists, park administrators, landowners, ranchers, local, regional, state and national politicians and legislators, professional and amateur lobbyists, wolf advocacy groups, environmentalists, ecologists, wilderness societies, sports hunters, lawyers, local residents and those who lived in distant cities. This was a momentous conservation issue: in the consultation period leading up to the publication of *The Final Environmental Impact Statement* in 1994, 750,000 documents were distributed, 700 witnesses testified at public hearings, and letters were received from all 50 US states as well as from 40 other countries. The recovery team also received 100,000 written comments favouring reintroduction and 60,000 opposing it. In a rather balanced way, Ed Bangs, the wolf specialist in charge of the team, described these 160,000 submissions as 'most of them, on both sides, misinformed'.[2] Not only was this a momentous conservation issue, it was the 'biggest official citizen response to any federal action, ever'.[3]

In the end eight wolves, captured in Canada, entered Yellowstone in purpose-built containers on 12 January 1995. Those opposed to the process fought against it with a last-minute legal appeal that prevented the wolves being allowed out of their containers, and the exhausted wolves were not released into their acclimatization pens until late the next day. Eight days later another six Canadian wolves joined them. On 21 March the pens were opened and the wolves slowly made their way into the park, in the hope that they might breed and populate Yellowstone once more.

It took twenty years of planning, analysis, debate, persuasion, anger, frustration, sometimes violence and hundreds of thousands of dollars for just a few wolves to be returned to the wilderness of Yellowstone. This can be seen as testimony to the powerful feelings, both for and against, that the wolf continues to provoke in human communities.

'Don't make a mistake!' educational poster issued by the US Government, c. 1990.

Elements of this story have been repeated in other countries and communities where the central conflict of modern wolf wars is not now a direct one of humans against wolves but rather a conflict between humans about wolves. Here wolves have symbolic power and come to represent bureaucratic, urban, central power imposing on marginalized, rural, powerless communities. In France, Spain, Italy and Greece, for example, pastoralists are angry that wolf numbers are increasing, yet they are not permitted to do anything about it. Their anger is directed against the wolves for their depredations on their flocks, but it is more forcibly directed against their governments and the conservation and environmental agencies that protect the wolf with anti-hunting or other anti-killing legislation, denying them the right to protect their own interests.[4] In the last few years a small number of wolves have emerged and begun to settle in Norway, from which they were eradicated through hunting in the nineteenth century. Although welcomed by many, particularly urban Norwegians who approve of them reinhabiting the wilderness, the arrival and right of residence of these newly protected wolves has been vigorously challenged by a range of rural interests. Sheep farmers, hunters, forest owners and others formed an anti-carnivore alliance to campaign against what they regarded as ill-conceived interference in rural affairs from urban-based conservation groups.[5] For modern pastoralists and other rural dwellers, the new enemy is often what they disparagingly term 'ecologists' and their powerful governmental allies.

Wolves are also seen as intruders. One of the complaints about the Yellowstone reintroduction was that the wolves were non-native, brought there from Canada. The wolves at the centre of the controversy in Norway are recent migrants from Sweden. The wolves that French shepherds protest against originally crossed into the country from Italy and Switzerland in the early 1990s. More recently in Germany wolves have moved into Saxony and Brandenburg from western Poland and now seem to be fully resident. In southern Albania, shepherds in the mountains of the Kurvelesh have spoken of how they not only have to contend with native wolves but also suffer depredations from wolves crossing the border from northern Greece, where they have thrived under the protection of Greek ecologists and environmentalists.

One of the few countries where there is no strong campaign against the wolf is Japan. Although the wolf is extinct there, Japanese farmers would like to see it reintroduced. Farmers have never been the greatest supporters of wolves, but most farmers in Japan are agriculturalists (rather than livestock farmers) who need to protect their crops from the ravages of wild boar and monkeys. Foresters must also protect their trees from serow and deer. Both groups must put a great deal of effort into keeping these crop-raiding animals at bay and and it is argued that the wolf would be a powerful weapon to control their numbers and impact. Beyond any utilitarian benefit, the possible reintroduction of wolves to Japan is also discussed in terms of a symbolic process of atonement for the sins of the destruction of wild environments in the pursuit of progress, the eradication of wolves because of human wrong-doing and deviation from traditional ways of engaging with the natural world.[6]

From among the Nez Perce people there came similar expressions of how the reintroduction of wolves signalled the possibility of a reconnection with lost cultural traditions and a renewal of a relationship with a quasi-sacred animal. In 1995 they became guardians and co-managers of a reintroduction project, closely linked with the Yellowstone experiment, in which 35 wolves were released onto their lands in neighbouring Idaho. Levi Holt, a

Nez Perce who worked on the project, believed that recovery of wolves would help his people and others to return to dignity and right ways of living.

> Restoring the wolf, protecting the wolf, sharing our lives with the wolf gives us a chance to have our culture re-born . . . We will honor our ancient relationships. What affects them affects us . . . We mourned your death. We were saddened by your exile. We rejoice in your return.[7]

Those who seek to keep the wolf at bay see themselves as the legitimate killers of wild animals that intrude in rapacious ways into human interests and concerns, whereas those who attempt to sponsor and protect wolves see themselves as the supporters of a creature that, through human self-interest, misunderstanding and cruelty, has been expelled from its proper place in the wild. Each group also has a view of the other. Pro-wolf activists regard the anti-wolf groups as heirs to a tradition that sought to subjugate and dominate the wild and fails to appreciate that the wild should have a value in and of itself. The anti-wolf activists regard their opponents as sentimental do-gooders who do not understand the complexities, and what they see as the realities, of rural life and who seek, from the safety of their urban centres, to impose an uncontrolled and threatening wild animal on those who have to live in proximity with it.

At the centre of human–wolf conflicts is not simply a wild animal that might, or might not, be allowed to live its own life on its own terms. Rather, it is *wolf*, a creature that must continue to carry the weight of its cultural creation. This wolf is a creature not just of flesh and blood and of its own habits but also a creature of human moral, social, economic, political, aesthetic and emotional concerns and projections. Such concerns will dictate, as they have for hundreds of years, whether wolves will be permitted to live and, if so, which wolves and how and where. The fate of the wolf is that it has always been a creature that is too powerful and potent for humans to ignore; its future depends on how people choose to pay attention to it.

Timeline of the Wolf

9–4.5 MYA	2.5–1.25 MYA	130,000–10,000 BC	2100–1200 BC	620–520 BC	42–39 BC
Emergence of *Canis* genus	Fossil evidence of first wolves	Dominance of *Canis lupus* among early wolf species	Compilation of *Gilgamesh*, early literary account of human-wolf transformation	Aesop's fables, including 'The Boy Who Cried Wolf'	Virgil's *Eclogues*, first literary account of voluntary werewolfery

Late 1600s	1758	*c.* 1770	1800s	1812	1826
Extinction of wolf in Scotland	The wolf is named *Canis lupus* by Linnaeus	Extinction of wolf in Ireland	Virtual extinction of wolves across Western Europe	Jacob and Wilhelm Grimm publish their version of 'Little Red Riding Hood'	Beginning of industrial production of Newhouse wolf traps at Oneida

1935	1936	1939	1941	1949	1963
The Werewolf of London, the beginning of Hollywood's fascination with werewolves	First performance of Prokofiev's *Peter and the Wolf*	Adolph Murie in Alaska begins the first scientific fieldwork on wolves	Formation, by Admiral Dönitz, of the German submarine 'wolf packs'	Publication of Leopold's book, in which he recounts his conversion from wolf hatred	Publication of *Never Cry Wolf*, a hugely influential account of the life of a wolf pack

29 BC	AD 812	Early 1500s	1589	1630	1697
Approximate date that Livy began his *History of Rome*, in which he recounts the legend of Romulus and Remus and the She-wolf	Charlemagne founds the Louveterie to kill wolves in royal forests	Extinction of the wolf in England	Peter Stumpf, the Werewolf of Bedburg, is executed	First wolf bounty in North America established by the Court of Assistants in Boston	Publication by Charles Perrault of the tale of 'Little Red Riding Hood'

1847	1894	1905	1915	1916	1920
Publication of George W. M. Reynolds's *Wagner, the Wehr-Wolf*, the first novel with a werewolf as the main character	Rudyard Kipling's *The Jungle Book* is published	The killing of probably the last wolf in Japan	First US federal funds for predator control in national parks	Foundation of the Wolf Cubs section of the Boy Scout Movement	The 'rescue' of Amala and Karmala from a wolf den in India

1972	1973	1990	1995	2010
Publication of Jean Craighead George's *Julie of the Wolves*, the first of a trilogy of books exploring the fictional relations between an Inupiat girl and a pack of wolves	Wolf protected by the Endangered Species Act in the United States. The Wolf Specialist Group of the International Union for the Conservation of Nature produces its first manifesto – Declaration of Principles for Wolf Conservation	Release of the film *Dances With Wolves*	Wolves are reintroduced into Yellowstone National Park	*The Wolfman*, remake of *The Werewolf of London* (1935)

References

INTRODUCTION

1 Georges-Louis Leclerc, Comte de Buffon, quoted in 'Canis', *Encyclopædia Britannica*, 3rd edn (Edinburgh, 1797), IV, p. 107.

1 *CANIS LUPUS*

1 See L. David Mech, *The Wolf: The Ecology and Behavior of an Endangered Species* (Minneapolis, MN, and London, 1970), a fine introduction to *Canis lupus*.
2 Ibid., p. 20.
3 The details in this section are taken from Ronald Novak, a specialist in wolf taxonomy. Ronald M. Nowak, 'Wolf Evolution and Taxonomy', in *Wolves: Behavior, Ecology, and Conservation*, ed. L. David Mech and Luigi Boitani (Chicago, IL, 2003).
4 I am indebted to classicist Frederick Ahl for this intriguing cultural observation.
5 Nowak, 'Wolf Evolution and Taxonomy'.
6 Mech, *The Wolf*, p. 12.
7 Barry Holstun Lopez, *Of Wolves and Men* (London, 1978), p. 18.
8 I am grateful to Professor Irina Chongarova for this translation.
9 Mech and Boitani, eds, *Wolves*, p. 32.
10 Ibid., p. 21.
11 Information concerning wolf communication is largely drawn from Harrington and Asa's extensive review of the literature. Fred H. Harrington and Cheryl S. Asa, 'Wolf Communication', in *Wolves*, ed. Mech and Boitani, pp. 66–103.

12 Rolf O. Petersson and Paola Ciucci, 'The Wolf as Carnivore', in *Wolves*, ed. Mech and Boitani, pp. 121–2.

13 L. David Mech, 'Whatever Happened to the Term Alpha Wolf', *International Wolf* (Winter 2008), pp. 4–7.

2 LUPOPHOBIA

1 Angela Carter, 'The Company of Wolves', in *The Bloody Chamber and Other Stories* (London, 1995), p. 111.

2 *Wolf Totem* (New York, 2008) by Lu Jiamin, but published under the pseudonym Jiang Rong, explores the intertwined lives of Mongolian herders and wolves during the 1960s at the time of the Maoist Cultural Revolution. Although the depictions of wolf lives are fanciful and far-fetched, the book does evoke the long history of the close connectedness of the herders with the natural world and the very different attitudes of the Han Chinese agricultural settlers who seek the total eradication of the wolf.

3 Isaiah 11:6.

4 Isaiah 65:25.

5 John 10:11–12.

6 Matthew 10:16.

7 Luke 10:3.

8 Matthew 7:15.

9 A. R. George, *The Babylonian Gilgamesh Epic*, vol. I (Oxford, 2003), p. 473.

10 In *Metaformations: Soundplay and Wordplay in Ovid and Other Classical Poets* (Ithaca, NY, and London, 1985), pp. 69–72, Frederick Ahl has a subtle and complex analysis of the linguistic plays of who or what was in the pot. He points out that the victim was a Molossian, suggesting a grinder (*mol*) of bones (*ossa*), a name used for a people who lived in Epirus who were famous for their fierce shepherding dogs (also known as Molossians). Perhaps the wolfish man was serving his arch enemy, the sheep-dog, as food.

11 Ovid, *Metamorphoses* (Oxford, 1986), 1.232–40.

12 Montague Summers, *The Werewolf in Lore and Legend* [1933] (New York, 2003), p. 65.

13 Virgil, *Eclogues* 8.96–100.

14 Petronius, *The Satyricon* (London, 1986), pp. 76–7.

15 Caroline Oates, 'Metamorphosis and Lycanthropy in Franche-Comté, 1521–1643', in *Fragments for a History of the Human Body*, ed. Michel Feher et al. (Cambridge, MA, 1989).

16 Oates, 'Metamorphosis and Lycanthropy', p. 321.

17 Charlotte Otten, ed., *A Lycanthropy Reader: Werewolves in Western Culture* (Syracuse, NY, 1986), p. 69.

18 Ibid., p. 72.

19 Ibid., p. 76.

20 Brian Frost, *The Essential Guide to Werewolf Literature* (Madison, WI, 2003).

21 Ibid., p. 173.

22 George W. M. Reynolds, *Wagner the Wehr-wolf* [1847] (Ware, 2006), p. 63.

23 *New York Times Review* (22 December 1941).

24 Personal communication with author.

25 Jack Zipes, ed., *The Trials and Tribulations of Little Red Riding Hood* (London, 1993).

26 Aleksander Pluskowski, *Wolves and the Wilderness in the Middle Ages* (Woodbridge, 2006), p. 11.

27 *New York Times* (19 March 1911).

28 Pluskowski, *Wolves and the Wilderness*, p. 41.

29 Homer, *The Iliad*, trans. Robert Fitzgerald (Oxford, 1998), 16.351–4.

30 Michael Speidel, *Ancient Germanic Warriors: Warrior Styles from Trajan's Column to Icelandic Sagas* (London, 2004), p 15.

31 Wolfgang Frank, *The Sea Wolves: The Story of the German U-Boats at War* (London, 1955), p. 73.

32 Material in this section is taken from Robert Waite, *The Psychopathic God: Adolf Hitler* (New York, 1977), especially pp. 26–7.

33 Viktor Suvorov, *Spetsnaz: The Story behind the Soviet SAS* (London, 1987), p. 38.

34 '"White Wolves" linked to Soho Bomb', BBC News online,
   30 April 1999.

3 LUPICIDE

1 For a detailed account of wolf eradication and later recovery, see
   Luigi Boitani, *Wolf Conservation and Recovery* (Chicago, IL, 2003).
2 William Wood, *New England's Prospect* (London, 1634), quoted in
   Peter Matthiessen, *Wildlife in America* (New York, 1987), p. 57.
3 Valerie Fogelman, 'American Attitudes towards Wolves: A History
   of Misconception', *Environmental Review*, 13 (1989), p. 66.
4 Ibid.
5 Jon T. Coleman, *Vicious: Wolves and Men in America* (New Haven,
   CT, 2004), pp. 9–10.
6 Rick McIntyre, ed., *War Against the Wolf: America's Campaign to
   Exterminate the Wolf* (Stillwater, MN, 1995), p. 30.
7 Stanley P. Young and Edward A. Goldman, *The Wolves of North
   America*, Part 1 [1944] (New York, 1964), p. 337.
8 Bruce Hampton, *The Great American Wolf* (New York, 1997),
   p. 67.
9 Young and Goldman, *The Wolves of North America*, p. 224.
10 Andrew Isenberg, *The Destruction of the Buffalo* (Cambridge,
   2000), p. 25.
11 L. C. Fouquet, 'Buffalo Days', *Kansas Historical Collections*, XVI
   (1925), p. 344.
12 Cited in Barry Lopez, *Of Wolves and Men* (New York, 1978), p. 181.
13 Brett Walker, *The Lost Wolves of Japan* (Seattle, WA, 2005), p. 131.
14 Ian M. Helfant, 'That Savage Gaze: The Contested Portrayal of
   Wolves in Nineteenth-century Russia', in *Other Animals: Beyond
   the Human in Russian Culture and History*, ed. Jane Costlow and
   Amy Nelson (Pittsburg, KS, 2010), p. 64. All the Russian material
   in this section has been taken from this chapter.
15 Roger Caras, *The Custer Wolf* (Harmondsworth, 1969), p. 108.
16 Stanley P. Young, *The Last of the Loners* (London, 1970), p. 114.
17 Ibid., p. 222.

18 Jon Coleman, *Vicious: Wolves and Men in America* (New Haven, CT, and London, 2004), p. 209.

19 Karen R. Jones, *Wolf Mountains: A History of Wolves along the Great Divide* (Calgary, AB, 2002).

20 Theodore Roosevelt, *The Wilderness Hunter* (New York, 1893), p. 386.

21 William Hornaday, *The American Natural History* (New York, 1904), p. 53.

22 William Hornaday, *The Minds and Manners of Wild Animals* (New York, 1922), p. 162.

4 LUPOPHILIA

1 Karl W. Luckert, *The Navajo Hunting Tradition* (Tucson, AZ, 1975), p. 51.

2 Richard K. Nelson, *Make Prayers to the Raven: A Koyukon View of the Northern Forest* (Chicago, IL, 1983), p. 159.

3 This material on Ainu relations with wolves has been taken from Brett Walker, *The Lost Wolves of Japan* (Seattle, WA, 2005), especially pp. 20 and 83–4. Walker's book is an extremely fine exploration of the complexities of attitudes to wolves historically and across the different cultures of Japan.

4 Joseph Marshall III, *On Behalf of the Wolf and the First Peoples* (Santa Fe, NM, 1995), p. 10.

5 Alice Henson Ernst, *Wolf Ritual of the Northwest Coast* [1952] (Eugene, OR, 2001), p. 3.

6 Titus Livius, *The History of Rome* (London, 1926), p. 6.

7 V. Ball, 'Wolf-reared Children', *Journal of the Royal Anthropological Institute of Great Britain and Ireland*, IX (1880), pp. 465–74.

8 Ibid., p. 473.

9 For debates relating to this issue see: Bruno Bettelheim, 'Feral Children and Autistic Children', *American Journal of Sociology*, LXIV/5 (1959), pp. 455–67; Wayne Dennis, 'A Further Analysis of Reports of Wild Children', *Child Development*, XXII/2 (1951), p. 158. For a full account of the case of Amala and Kamala see Charles Maclean, *The Wolf Children: Fact or Fantasy?* (London,

1979). The website FeralChildren.com has extracts from Singh's
   diary and many other cases of wolf-children.

10 John Lockwood Kipling, *Man and Beast in India: A Popular Sketch
   of Indian Animals and their Relations with People* (London, 1904),
   p. 281.

11 Rudyard Kipling, *The Jungle Book* [1894] (London, 1947), p. 10.

12 Robert Baden-Powell, *Wolf Cub's Handbook* (London, 1958),
   p. 32.

13 Brian Morris, 'Ernest Thompson Seton and the Origins of the
   Woodcraft Movement', *Journal of Contemporary History*, V/2
   (1970), pp. 183–94.

14 Ibid., p. 187.

15 Roderick Nash, 'The American Cult of the Primitive', *American
   Quarterly*, XVIII/3 (1970), p. 522.

16 Ibid.

17 For a popular account of the work of key wolf researchers, see
   Mike Link and Kate Crowley, *Following the Pack: The World of Wolf
   Research* (Stillwater, MN, 1994).

18 Adolph Murie, *The Wolves of Mount McKinley* [1944] (Seattle,
   WA, 2001), p. xiii.

19 Ibid., p. 232.

20 When David Mech and Luigi Boitani (if Mech is synonymous
   with wolf studies in North America, Boitani is the wolfman of
   European studies) published their comprehensive edited volume
   Wolves: Behavior, Ecology, and Conservation (Chicago, IL, 2003),
   the lives of wolves was captured in thirteen major essays that
   were supported by references to some 1,600 books and articles
   of wolf research.

21 Link and Crowley, *Following the Pack*, p. 19.

22 Aldo Leopold, *A Sand County Almanac* [1949] (Oxford, 1966),
   p. 138.

23 Farley Mowat, *Never Cry Wolf* (Toronto, 1993), p. 60.

24 Ibid., p. viii.

25 For a full exploration of the social, cultural and scientific debates
   about *Never Cry Wolf* and its status as an early environmental text,

see Karen Jones, '"Never Cry Wolf": Science, Sentiment and the Literary Rehabilitation of *Canis lupus*', *Canadian Historical Review*, LXXXIV/1 (2003), pp. 65–93.

26 Ibid, pp. 65–9.

27 L. David Mech, *The Wolf: The Ecology and Behavior of an Endangered Species* (Minneapolis, MN, and London, 1970), p. 340.

28 Personal communication with author.

29 For a fine survey of how wolves have been represented in modern children's fiction, see Peter Hollingdale, 'Why the Wolves are Running', *The Lion and the Unicorn*, XXIII/1 (1999), pp. 97–115.

30 For a superb review of classic and modern stories, see Debra Mitts-Smith, *Picturing the Wolf in Children's Literature* (New York and London, 2010).

31 Laurence Anholt and Arthur Robins, *Eco-Wolf and the Three Pigs* (London, 2002).

32 Bob Hartman and Tim Raglin, *The Wolf Who Cried Boy* (Oxford, 2003).

33 Angela Carter, 'The Company of Wolves', *The Bloody Chamber and Other Stories* (London, 1995), p. 118.

34 Clarissa Pinkola Estés, *Women Who Run With Wolves* (London, 1992), p. 2.

35 Ibid.

36 Ibid., p. 24.

37 Michael Blake, *Dances With Wolves* (London, 1988), p. 120.

38 Ibid., pp. 201–2.

39 The text of this new Peter and the Wolf story can be found at www.russianarts.org (accessed 17 March 2011).

40 For the website and the game go to www.wolfquest.org (accessed 17 March 2011).

41 Wolf places that seem to have earned a high reputation for encouraging new attitudes to wolves and an immediate experience of wolves would include the International Wolf Center in Minnesota, the Lakota Wolf Preserve in New Jersey, the UK Wolf Conservation Trust and Les Loups du Gévaudan in Ménatory,

France. Scores of others can be found by entering a phrase such as 'seeing wolves up close' into an Internet search engine.

42 Peter A. Coates, 'The Strange Stillness of the Past: Toward an Environmental History of Sound and Noise', *Environmental History* (October 2005), par. 31.

43 Stanley P. Young and Edward A. Goldman, *The Wolves of North America*, Part 1 [1944] (New York, 1964), p. 76.

44 Bruce Hampton, *The Great American Wolf*, p. 169.

5 REWILDING

1 Anita Endrezze, 'Return of the Wolves', in *At the Helm of Twilight* (Seattle, WA, 1992).

2 Thomas McNamee, *The Return of the Wolf to Yellowstone* (New York, 1997), p. 45.

3 Ibid.

4 See Henry Buller, 'Safe from the Wolf: Biosecurity, Biodiversity and Competing Philosophies of Nature', *Economy and Planning A*, 40 (2008), pp. 1583–97, and Ketil Skogen, Isabelle Mauz and Olve Krange, 'Cry Wolf! Narratives of Wolf Recovery in France and Norway', *Rural Sociology*, LXXIII/3 (2008), pp. 105–33, for analyses of the complexities surrounding the reappearance of wolves.

5 For a fuller discussion of the issues, see Ketil Skogen and Olve Krange, 'A Wolf at the Gate: The Anti-Carnivore Alliance and the Symbolic Construction of Community', *Sociologica Ruralis*, XLIII/3 (2003), pp. 309–25.

6 The complexities of the arguments about whether wolves ought to be in Japan and why are discussed in John Knight, *Waiting for Wolves in Japan: An Anthropological Study of People–Wildlife Relations* (Oxford, 2003).

7 Quoted in Catherine Feher-Elston, *Wolf Song: A Natural and Fabulous History of Wolves* (New York, 2004), pp. 169–70.

Select Bibliography

Two books will be essential further reading for anyone interested in wolves. Barry Lopez's *Of Wolves and Men* (London, 1978) is a now classic study of how wolves have figured in human cultures. David Mech and Luigi Boitani, eds, *Wolves: Behavior, Ecology, and Conservation* (Chicago, IL, 2003) is the most comprehensive and authoritative single-volume account of the biology, behaviour and social ecology of the wolf. It also deals with conservation and human–wolf relations issues.

Bergman, Charles, *Wild Echoes: Encounters with the Most Endangered Animals in North America* (Urbana and Chicago, IL, 2003)

Blake, Michael, *Dances With Wolves* (London, 1998)

Coleman, Jon, *Vicious: Wolves and Men in America* (New Haven, CT, 2004)

Craighead George, Jean, *Julie of the Wolves* (New York, 1972)

——, *Julie* (New York, 1994)

——, *Julie's Wolf Pack* (New York, 1997)

Feher-Elston, Catherine, *Wolf Song: A Natural and Fabulous History of Wolves* (New York, 2004)

Fischer, Hank, *Wolf Wars: The Remarkable Inside Story of the Restoration of Wolves to Yellowstone* (Missoula, MT, 2003)

Frost, Brian, *The Essential Guide to Werewolf Literature* (Madison, WI, 2003)

Hampton, Bruce, *The Great American Wolf* (New York, 1997)

Hornaday, William, *The American Natural History* (New York, 1904)

——, *The Minds and Manners of Wild Animals* (New York, 1902)

Jones, Karen R., *Wolf Mountains: A History of Wolves Along the Great Divide* (Calgary, AB, 2002)

Kipling, Rudyard, *The Jungle Book* [1894] (London 1947)

Knight, John, *Waiting for Wolves in Japan: An Anthropological Study of People-Wildlife Relations* (Cambridge, 2003)

Leopold, Aldo, *A Sand County Almanac* (Oxford, 1966)

Link, Mike, and Kate Crowley, *Following the Pack: The World of Wolf Research* (Stillwater, MN, 1994)

Maclean, Charles, *The Wolf Children: Fact or Fantasy?* (London, 1979)

Mazzoni, Cristina, *She-Wolf: The Story of a Roman Icon* (Cambridge, 2010)

McIntyre, Rick, ed., *War Against the Wolf: America's Campaign to Exterminate the Wolf* (Stillwater, MN, 1995)

McNamee, Thomas, *The Return of the Wolf to Yellowstone* (New York, 1997)

Mech, L. David, *The Wolf: The Ecology and Behavior of an Endangered Species*, (Minneapolis, MN, 1970)

Mitts-Smith, Debra, *Picturing the Wolf in Children's Literature* (New York and London, 2010).

Mowat, Farley, *Never Cry Wolf* (Toronto, ON, 1993)

Murie, Adolph, *The Wolves of Mount McKinley* [1944] (Seattle, WA, 2001)

Nelson, Richard K., *Make Prayers to the Raven: A Koyukon View of the Northern Forest* (Chicago, IL, 1986)

Otten, Charlotte, ed., *A Lycanthropy Reader: Werewolves in Western Culture* (Syracuse, NY, 1986)

Pluskowski, Aleksander, *Wolves and the Wilderness in the Middle Ages* (Woodbridge, 2006)

Reynolds, George W. M., *Wagner the Wehr-wolf* [1847] (Ware, 2006)

Robisch, S. K., *Wolves and the Wolf Myth in American Literature*, (Reno, NV, 2009)

Rong, Jiang, *Wolf Totem* (New York, 2008)

Singh, J.A.L., and Robert Zingg, *Wolf Children and Feral Man* (New York, 1942)

Summers, Montague, *The Werewolf in Lore and Legend* [1933] (New York, 2003)

Walker, Brett, *The Lost Wolves of Japan* (Seattle, WA, 2005)
Young, Stanley Paul, *The Last of the Loners* (London, 1970)
Zipes, Jack, ed., *The Trials and Tribulations of Little Red Riding Hood* (London, 1993)

Associations and Websites

www.wolfsongaslaska.org
Established in 1988, Wolf Song Alaska is an organization committed
to understanding both the natural and the cultural history of the wolf.

www.wolf.org
This is the website of the International Wolf Center in Ely,
Minnesota. It contains a searchable database of in-depth resources,
sections on the status of wolves in different countries and webcams
of the wolves at the centre.

www.defenders.org
Defenders of Wildlife is an advocacy and campaigning organization
based in Washington, DC. The website offers access to important
documents relating to the state and status of wolves in the US and
other parts of the world.

www.ukwcf.uk
The UK Wolf Conservation Trust. The website offers access to
information about their projects, to a wide literature on wolves
and links to further wolf-related sites.

Acknowledgements

My first thanks must go to Jonathan Burt, who continued to give his support despite the long, unforgivably long, gestation period of this book. Also to Michael Leaman, Blanche Craig and Susannah Jayes, who finally shaped it for publication. My sincere thanks to Peter Coates and Jules Pretty, who read early drafts and made invaluable comments and offered fine advice. My warm thanks to Fred Ahl for his advice and instruction in all things classical and animally. Erica Fudge and Donna Landry went way beyond responding to the call of a friend asking for their comments on this manuscript. Both of them took their finely honed intellectual scalpels to it paragraph by paragraph, cutting through weak arguments and flabby constructions. I am greatly indebted to them. Finally my deep gratitude to Stephanie Schwandner-Sievers, who has lived with this far too long, has read too many drafts and listened patiently to the howls of despair in the house. This book is for Imogen Schwander and Nicola Schwander; both daughters of sorts.

Photo Acknowledgements

The author and the publishers wish to thanks to the below sources of illustrative material and/or permission to reproduce it. (Some sources uncredited in the captions for reasons of brevity are also given below.)

123rf Stock Photos: p. 51 (Remi Callens); Bodleian Library, University of Oxford: p. 54; Vladimir Bologov: pp. 28, 32; © The Trustees of the British Museum: pp. 17, 36, 46, 73, 121, 128, 133; The Detroit Institute of Arts: p. 124; © Grupo Lobo: p. 102 (Francisco Álvares); Istockphoto: p. 169 (Chris Alcock); Library of Congress: pp. 77, 114, 127; The Metropolitan Museum of Art: p. 86; The Minneapolis Institute of Art: p. 120; National Park Service US Department of the Interior: pp. 19, 22, 24–5, 29–31 (all Doug Smith); Scala Archives: p. 129; The Smithsonian Museum of Art: p. 125; Topkapi Museum, Istanbul: p. 38; US Fish and Wildlife Services: p. 6 (Steve Hillebrand); Zoological Society of London: pp. 18, 57.

Index

Aesop 38–40

Baden-Powell, Robert 137, 138
Boy Scout movement 137–9
buffalo and wolves 97–100
Buffon, Comte de 7

Carter, Angela 35, 152–3
Charlemagne 81
Christian imagery 40–46, 53,
    59, 87
Coates, Peter 167
colonial encounters 85–94
Craighead George, Jean 148–9
Cromwell, Oliver 82

Dances with Wolves 155–8

Edgar, English King 81
Endrezze, Anita 172
eradication of wolves
    bounties 81, 82, 89–92, 95, 104
    hunting 82, 104
    poison 96, 100, 104
    traps 83, 96, 107–9

Endangered Species Act 86,
    117, 175

Gilgamesh 46

Hitler, Adolf 76
Hornaday, William 115
human–wolf conflict 35–7, 84–6,
    100–116, 174, 178

Iliad, The 73
India 131–4
infamous wolves 109–11

Japan 102–3, 121
Jones, Karen 146
Jungle Book, The 134–7

Kipling, John Lockwood 134
Kipling, Rudyard 134
Koyukon people 120

Lakota people 122
Leopold, Aldo 143–4
Linnaeus, Carl 13

Livy 127
Lycaon 47

Marshall III, Joseph 122
Mather, Cotton 88
Mech, David 11, 32, 142,
    146
Mowat, Farley 144–8
Mowgli 134–7
Murie, Adolph 141

national parks, 115–17, 166,
    168–70, 175–7
Navajo 'Hunting Way' 119,
    120
Nelson, Richard 120
Newhouse, Sewell 107
Nez Perce people 179–80

Oates, Caroline 53
Olson, Sigurd 141

Peter and the Wolf 162–4
Petronius 50
Pimlott, Doug 142
Pinkola Estés, Clarissa 152–5
Pluskowski, Aleksander 70, 72

Red Riding Hood 64–70
reintroductions 172–9
Reynolds, George 58
rituals 123–6
Romulus and Remus 127–31
Roosevelt, Theodore 115
Russia 72, 103–4

sexual imagery 70, 71
sheep's clothing 46
Sonny, Claus Chee 119
Stumpf, Peter 56–7
Summers, Montague 49

Thompson Seton, Ernest 110, 139

U-boats 75

Virgil 49

warriors 74, 78
werewolves 48–64
wilderness 159
Winthrop, John 88
Wolf children 127–34
wolf
    emergence of species 11–15
    breeding 20, 22
    communication 26
    den 21
    family structure 20, 33
    hierarchy 31–4
    howling 24–7, 167–71
    hunting 27–31,
    lone wolves 23
    pack 19
    parenting 21–2
    size 15
    social life 20, 23
    teeth 16
    territory 21, 23